CONRAD,

THANK YOU FOR YOUR
HELP WITH THIS BOOK.
IT WAS A BLAST TALKING
TO YOU, AND I HOPE YOUR
READERS ENJOY YOUR
STORIES AS MUCH AS
I DID.

SINCERELY,

JOHN McFARLAND

Glenn

I am sure you will enjoy
this much more. I wrote a
chapter.

Connie

D1416492

# FACING AMERICA'S TEAM

PLAYERS RECALL THE GLORY YEARS OF THE DALLAS COWBOYS

EDITED BY JOHN McFARLAND

SPORTS
PUBLISHING

Sports Publishing books may be purchased in bulk at special discounts for sales promotion, corporate gifts, fund-raising, or educational purposes. Special editions can also be created to specifications. For details, contact the Special Sales Department, Sports Publishing, 307 West 36th Street, 11th Floor, New York, NY 10018 or sportspubbooks@skyhorsepublishing.com.

Sports Publishing® is a registered trademark of Skyhorse Publishing, Inc.®, a Delaware corporation.

Visit our website at www.sportspubbooks.com.

10 9 8 7 6 5 4 3 2 1

Library of Congress Cataloging-in-Publication Data is available on file.

Cover design by Tom Lau
Cover photo credit AP Images

ISBN: 978-1-61321-807-5
Ebook ISBN: 978-1-61321-843-3

Printed in the United States of America

For Lori, Mason, and Riley

# CONTENTS

# FACING AMERICA'S TEAM

# INTRODUCTION

**VERY FEW PEOPLE** know what it's really like to play in the NFL. Fewer yet know what it felt like to take on the greatest Dallas Cowboys: to block Bob Lilly, chase Roger Staubach, tackle Emmitt Smith, or get clobbered by Larry Allen.

*Facing America's Team* brings you a sense of those challenges through the firsthand stories, memories, and observations of 80 of the Dallas Cowboys' opponents over the years. These Dallas foes, including 20 Hall of Famers, describe Super Bowls, conference championships, historic plays, bitter rivalries, and even Pro Bowls. In short, they know America's Team very well.

They played during the greatest eras in Cowboys history, from the team's rise to power in the 1960s, through the 20 straight winning seasons that included five Super Bowls in the 1970s, up to the overpowering 1990s teams that captured three Lombardi Trophies in four years. Some opponents detailed key moments like they were yesterday. Some told funny stories. Some talked very strategically. Some described how the Cowboys behaved on the field. Most respected the Cowboys, but some didn't like them very much. (Some even cussed a little. Sorry, kids.)

Now, let's take a look at the Cowboys all these guys are talking about. The 24 Dallas greats highlighted in these pages were selected using a very simple formula: Those in the Pro Football Hall of Fame were automatics. Then came those in the Ring of Honor who also won Super Bowls. The field was expanded slightly to include the players they are naturally connected with; after all, you can't include Cliff Harris without Charlie Waters, you can't list Randy White but not

Harvey Martin and Ed "Too Tall" Jones, and you can't have Larry Allen without his mean and nasty buddies.

Listening to familiar Cowboys tales from a different perspective was a lot of fun. And there were plenty of tidbits I'd never heard. Discussions with these former Dallas opponents often strayed to cover a wide array of years, stadiums, games, and vivid moments. I edited their tales to keep them concise and focused on the players they were discussing. Because these Dallas rivals took on many Cowboys, you'll encounter some of them in various areas of the book—including the "Extra Points" and "Overtime" sections, which are made up of stories, quotes, and tidbits that were too good to be left out. I hope you enjoy reading their stories as much as I enjoyed collecting them.

# Section 1
# The Foundation

THE DALLAS COWBOYS started the way most expansion teams do—they were terrible. With a first-year roster composed largely of castoffs, rookies, and broken-down old-timers, the 1960 Cowboys turned in an embarrassing 0-11-1 debut season. Yet for all they lacked on the field, they sure were stacked in key leadership positions.

Coach/football genius Tom Landry engineered a disciplined defensive scheme and installed an innovative offense. Vice president of player personnel Gil Brandt found the right players to make the system go, thanks to an ahead-of-its-time computerized scouting system and his knack for discovering stars where few other teams looked. President and General Manager Tex Schramm brought the media savvy and marketing skills to turn the Cowboys into a big-time franchise.

Before long the Cowboys were a contender. They made the playoffs for the first time in 1966, launching an incredible run of 20 straight winning seasons. They came within a touchdown of making the first AFL-NFL World Championship Game (as the Super Bowl was initially known). The next year they again challenged Green Bay for the NFL crown, only to lose in the final seconds of the famous Ice Bowl. By the close of the 1960s, the foundation for America's Team was taking shape, with sturdy building blocks who would pay dividends for years to come: Bob Lilly, Chuck Howley, Lee Roy Jordan, Mel Renfro, Bob Hayes, and Rayfield Wright.

# CHAPTER 1

# FACING BOB LILLY

---

**Defensive Tackle (1961–74), No. 74**
**Pro Football Hall of Fame, Dallas Cowboys Ring of Honor**

**B**OB LILLY COMES by the nickname "Mr. Cowboy" honestly: He was the team's first-ever draft pick, the first Cowboy named to the Pro Football Hall of Fame, and the first member of the team's Ring of Honor. He played on the first Dallas team to reach the Super Bowl and the first to win it all. The 6-foot-5 native Texan was wiry, quick, intense, strong, and smart, earning a reputation very early on as a guy who could blow up the interior of an offensive line. He won Rookie of the Year honors and soon was the centerpiece of the Doomsday Defense—so dominant that he made the All-Decade team for both the 1960s and 1970s. Lilly never missed a regular-season game in 14 years, and he still owns the club record for most consecutive games played. His No. 74 is the only jersey the team has retired.

# Tom Mack

## Hall of Fame Guard

*Team: Los Angeles Rams, 1966–78*
*His View: The Rams and Cowboys were usually among the top teams from the mid-1960s through the 1970s, so when Lilly and Mack clashed their games meant something. The battles with Lilly were always tough, Mack recalls, because their strengths were very similar.*

**H**E WAS THE best defensive tackle I ever played against, and I tell people that all the time. He had the great quickness and agility. And he was an extremely disciplined player, so you had to anticipate what he was going to do.

He was never the kind of player who would try to run over you. Randy White would try to run over you. But Bob was more of a guy who would get the angle, get you turned off balance, get by you that way. When we played Dallas, I spent more time than usual getting ready to play. I always tried to concentrate on his best shot because people are predictable and will go for their best one before moving on to the next one. I managed to do that. I had some pretty good games against Bob.

Today, pass-blocking is so different. You're basically being paid to grab the guy and pull him to you, like a Sumo wrestler. They reach out and grab the defender and it looks like two guys dancing, if you watch it closely. When we played, for the most part you had to keep your hands closed in a fist. And you'd punch a guy to make him restart. If you hit him twice there was no way he was getting to the quarterback. The good defensive tackles and ends would get to the side. Merlin Olsen would get to your side. Bob got to your side. Deacon Jones got to your side.

I think Bob had a lot of respect for me, and I consider him a good friend now and I think he'd consider me a good friend. So it's funny how it works out. But he sure was a handful.

# Bill Curry

## Center

*Teams: Green Bay Packers, 1965–66; Baltimore Colts, 1967–72; Houston Oilers, 1973; Los Angeles Rams, 1974*

*His View: Curry knew what to expect from Lilly in the Cowboys' first Super Bowl, after the 1970 season. Curry had faced him plenty both as the Colts' center and as a member of Vince Lombardi's Packers.*

**H**E WAS A force of nature. He was wiry, but you couldn't knock him back. When you tried to smash him, he'd go around you. He was fast; he was so fast. And he was intense. He never said a word on the field. He didn't talk trash, didn't grimace, didn't smile. Nothing.

In Green Bay, we had some great players—some really great players—who would come back to the bench and say, "I can't block Lilly." I'd say, "You have to," and they'd say, "But I can't." You couldn't run a play without having a provision for him. Lombardi would change everything we had been doing when we faced Dallas. We would reverse all our tendencies. Of course, it was against all of them, but the main figure was number 74.

In the Super Bowl against Dallas, we didn't have a lot of plays on offense. It was embarrassing. Whatever we did, it didn't work. We had systems in place so Lilly wouldn't take over. But you can't always get all wrapped up in doubling him, especially if there are great players all over the defense. There wasn't a lot to do to dominate him—draw plays, traps—whatever we did, it didn't work.

The best play I ever had against him was when I was running down the line and looking over my shoulder to see if somebody was coming.

Bob was sprinting right down the line of scrimmage with the back, and he didn't see me. I hit him and got just enough to knock him down. That was my only one-on-one block I remember. A true one-on-one between him and me would have been very bad for me.

I remember one time, Cornelius Johnson, our backup guard in Baltimore, was playing him in an exhibition game. Cornelius always got nauseated when he was going to play. I was lined up next to him and he threw up a little bit and started gagging. Lilly picked his hands up and backed off. We did good on that play, so we asked Corny if he could do that all the time against Bob.

# Paul Warfield

## Hall of Fame Wide Receiver

*Teams:* *Cleveland Browns, 1964–69, 1976–77; Miami Dolphins, 1970–74*
*His View:* *The Cowboys held the Dolphins to just a field goal when they won their first Super Bowl after the 1971 season. That was the fewest points ever scored by the loser of a Super Bowl. Lilly set the defensive tone in the first quarter with a wild pursuit of Bob Griese that ended in a sack for a 29-yard loss.*

**I WAS DOWNFIELD, TRYING** to do what I was supposed to be doing, and I turned when I was at the breaking point looking for the pass that was going to come my way.

It was obvious that pressure had occurred in the pocket, and Bob Griese had been flushed out of there. At that point, a receiver is coached to break whatever pattern that had been called in the huddle and just try to find an open spot on the field.

As I was looking back in that direction, Bob was under tremendous pressure from the Cowboy defensive front and of course Bob Lilly. While Bob was weaving and trying to get away, Bob Lilly—being the great defensive player he was—turned it into a phenomenal loss. Plays like that, the Cowboys made seemingly all day long.

# Conrad Dobler

## Guard

*Teams: St. Louis Cardinals, 1972–77; New Orleans Saints, 1978–79; Buffalo Bills, 1980–81*
*His View: For much of his 10-year career, Dobler managed to avoid Lilly. He usually played right guard, away from Lilly, but wasn't so fortunate when he lined up on the other side during his rookie season.*

**I HAD AN ADVANTAGE** because I was new to the league and there was no film on me, but I had seen plenty of film on him. Going in, I knew he was the best I was going to play against that year so I was fired up for it. I kind of had a good game against him. There were times when he really thought he had me beat, but in reality he didn't. They came out on top, of course. We didn't win a lot of games that year.

They played that Flex defense, so sometimes one tackle would be up on one guard and the other would be way back off the other guard by about a yard. They did a lot of reading of the offensive line. When Bob Lilly was off the ball, or set off to the right or left, you really didn't have much of a chance of getting into him or squaring up with him. That's the way the Flex defense was made, not allowing you to square up against defensive linemen.

Somehow Bob would stay low. Bob never let you get into his body too much. He was light of foot. If you'd get to the right of him, he'd spin off and next thing you know he's on your left. If you planted your feet to take him on, he was going to beat you.

He was a real technician. He kept his poise during the game. You couldn't get Bob Lilly out of his game. One way to take a guy out of his game is to knock him off the ball and make sure he could never get to the quarterback. That's pretty discouraging for a player. But against Bob, you had your hands full.

Bob was just quick with his hands, almost like Bruce Lee. He'd get his hands up and never let you get to his body. I think I was really happy to get through the game and maybe only give up one sack to him. To me that was a success.

## Billy Kilmer

### Quarterback

**Teams:** *San Francisco 49ers, 1961–66; New Orleans Saints, 1967–70; Washington Redskins, 1971–78*

**His View:** *Kilmer first met Lilly when they were both college kids, for television appearances and sightseeing with the 1960 All-America team in New York. (Lilly was introduced by the name of Robert Lilly, which Kilmer calls him to this day.) Once in the NFL, Kilmer's fun times with Robert Lilly were over.*

WHEN YOU TALK about the NFL, everyone's quick and everybody's strong and everything, but the thing about Robert was he was a very intelligent football player. He studied the game pretty good. He'd look at a lineman's hands and know that if he had white knuckles that meant the guy was coming at him and if the was laying off a bit that meant he was going to pull. Robert would look at things like that. He'd pick up things. You couldn't give away a lot of stuff. You couldn't signal a lot of things before the snap.

On running downs you really had to double-team him because he'd shoot that gap so fast. And you had to change the count up on him because if you had consistency on the count, he could destroy a running game. I used to try to throw on first down a lot because they were playing the run.

He was always in your hair. I remember playing against him when I was with the New Orleans Saints, and we didn't have very good teams back then. You talk about Lilly being quick; he would get through my guards and I was running for my life back in those days.

# John Wooten

## Guard

*Teams: Cleveland Browns, 1959–67; Washington Redskins, 1968*
*His View: Long before his 17-year career as a scout and director of player personnel in Dallas, Wooten lined up against Lilly twice a year when the Browns and Cowboys were division rivals. He spent most of his career trying to move Lilly, one of the greatest defensive tackles ever, in order to make running room for Jim Brown, one of the greatest running backs ever.*

**F**IRST AND FOREMOST, Lilly had unbelievable quickness. I don't see any player today nor have I ever seen a defensive lineman with the quickness of Bob Lilly—and I've scouted for years and years. He couldn't outrun a lot of people in the 40, but he had that outstanding quickness that makes a defensive lineman hard to block.

One of the other things that made him outstanding was that he played in that four-point stance and he would crowd the ball tremendously. Our center, John Morrow, had a tendency to put the ball further up under him. The line of scrimmage is the football, so consequently putting that ball up under him created problems for me. So I'm saying, "John, get the ball out of there; put it out front!"

And Dallas played that defense. Nobody today plays the Flex. And the reason they don't play it is because they don't know how to teach it. It was an unbelievable defense. We always played down in Texas when the State Fair was going at the Cotton Bowl, for whatever reason. And it was hot. We had to just prepare for the heat, the Flex, and all of those outstanding defensive players.

Jim Brown had some pretty outstanding games against them. But by the same token there were some times when we didn't have any good yardage running the football. So it was probably a pretty even battle over the years.

We had a couple of trap plays that we relied on, but we knew we weren't going to be able to trap Lilly because of where he played on the line. So what we came up with was the option block, where both John Morrow and I would both come right at him, straight up. If he stayed where he was, we were going to double-team him and drive him out of there. Or if he was knifing down inside, then John would take him and I'd slip through and get on the linebacker. When we were able to use the option block, Bob didn't know which one of us was going to take him. So there were plays we had to give up on against him, but there were plays we had success with.

Lilly had some very good games against me. I don't know if I gave up so many sacks, but I know we were off balance trying to keep him off of our quarterback Frank Ryan. But Frank understood he couldn't sit back there, and he had to get that ball out of there. I don't know if there were any days when I was just devastated by him. We had some good football games, where he won some battles and I won some battles. Overall, what I thoroughly enjoyed was the fact that we beat the Cowboys more than they beat us when I played.

You never heard Lilly hollering and cursing. A lot of the defensive players would say, "Oh, you're holding me, you're this, you're that . . ." but you never heard him say any of that. He just played hard. If you were able to get a block on him, he'd say, "Hey, great block."

Lilly comes across as a very quiet guy, but he is a definite talker. He can talk to you about a lot of things. In the years going to the Pro Bowl, I really got to know him as a person. He's an outstanding person.

There's a reason why they called him Mr. Cowboy. He fully exemplifies everything we think of when you think of a cowboy: tough, rugged, fair play, standing up for what is right all the time. I have great respect for him. He was truly a great football player and is just an ideal person.

# Ray Schoenke

## Guard

*Teams: Dallas Cowboys, 1963–64; Washington Redskins, 1966–75*
*His View: Schoenke was a defensive lineman when the Cowboys drafted him out of SMU, so he arrived envisioning himself chasing quarterbacks alongside Lilly. Instead, Coach Tom Landry turned him into an offensive lineman. Schoenke later joined the hated Redskins and lined up directly across from Lilly twice a year.*

WHEN I CAME in to Dallas, I didn't even know how to pass-block. I was trying to block Lilly in practice and he was running all around me every which way. I could barely get a hand on him. So I grabbed his facemask and threw him down and that started a big fight. Finally, Jim Ray Smith took me aside and showed me some pass-blocking techniques. It took me a while to figure it out.

My first start in Washington was about midway through the season against Dallas. It was going to be against Lilly, and I knew that would make me or break me, so I began an intense study of him to figure out why he was so great. I looked at all his tendencies and what he did well. I really had the book on him.

He could somehow grab the quarterback before he even faded back. He'd be in a four-point stance, and then he could just spring like a cat. He could sometimes grab three people at a time—the quarterback, guard, and center. He just disrupted everything. His job was to take the center and me away so nobody could get to the linebacker. So I worked very hard to figure out Lilly. I tried to take away his quick inside move. His number-one move was to go between the center and guard and disrupt that gap. I knew he was always going to do this.

After one game a reporter went to him and said, "Ray Schoenke got a game ball against you." He said, "Tell Ray he's never going to get another game ball against me." He suddenly developed an outside move against me, and that changed everything. I had to respect his outside move, and it was a lot tougher.

I eventually figured out how to take away that first leap he had. I backed off the line so he couldn't grab me to start and I could watch him. I also had to beat him on the count. If I could get a half-second head start on him, I had a chance.

Lilly was naturally strong. He didn't lift weights. And he went the same speed on the first play all the way to the last play of the game. He was so great that other players would try to copy him. It was great to play against him, though, because it made me rise to another level. He was by far the best player I ever played against.

# Norm Bulaich

## Running Back

*Teams: Baltimore Colts, 1970–72; Philadelphia Eagles, 1973–74; Miami Dolphins, 1975–79*

*His View: The burly Bulaich fully expected to run over the Cowboys in Super Bowl V. Even though he was just a rookie, none other than Johnny Unitas told him he'd get 20 carries. He nearly did, but it hurt: Bulaich ran 18 times for only 28 yards. In one series, he was stopped at the Dallas 2 for no gain on three straight runs.*

**M**Y FIRST PLAYOFF game was against Cincinnati and I gained 116 yards, and then I scored two touchdowns against Oakland to take us into the Super Bowl. I thought, "Heck, I'm pretty good." Then the Super Bowl came and, obviously, I got killed. Whether it be Bob Lilly or Lee Roy Jordan or Chuck Howley or Jethro Pugh, I just got beat up.

I remember running a sweep. Lilly used to follow the guards out whenever they would pull, and I remember cutting back up the field and I ran right into Bob. He was lying on top of me after hitting me hard, and I was thinking, "We both played at TCU, so he'll help me up." Then he put his fist in my chest and helped himself up, so I knew he was serious about this.

We couldn't run. I remember our guard Glenn Ressler, who never said anything to anybody, he comes over to me and says, "Why don't you get through the hole?" I said, "Why don't you open a hole?" I kept saying, "Open one, and I'll get through one." We were just tossing that back and forth the whole game.

Bob just read the whole offense. He had a lot of finesse and always knew how to get to the quarterback or running back. I asked Lilly, sometime after the game: "What'd y'all do?" And he said, "You know Landry; he knows how to stop a running back's momentum."

I was going to shake his hand after the game, and when I saw him throw his helmet into the air and it went flying, I thought: "I'm not going over there. I won't bother him at this moment."

# Bill Lueck

## Guard

*Teams: Green Bay Packers, 1968–74; Philadelphia Eagles, 1975*
*His View: The first time he faced Lilly, Lueck was a rookie backup who was only playing because of an injury to Jerry Kramer—a hero of the Ice Bowl against Dallas the year before. The Packers won this meeting, too, and the Lueck vs. Lilly matchup went about how you'd expect.*

**T**HAT'S WHEN I got my baptism against Bob Lilly. And it wasn't a very fun day. Not a good day at all. I can put it very simply for you: I got my ass kicked.

What Bob would do was grab you behind your shoulder pads and get your body turned to where you couldn't stay square. Once your shoulder gets turned, he'd use that swim move and get right by you.

The guy had great footwork for a guy his size. He's the one who gave me the most trouble. I played against Alan Page. He was difficult, but he didn't have the same strength of Bob Lilly. You could usually get even with him. Bob Lilly could make you look like an idiot. He could really embarrass you.

The difference in the game in those days was the head slap. It was legal then. If you've ever been slapped upside the head, it's not a good thing. Besides the fact your ears are going to be ringing, it knocks you off balance. So there was a little head slap and a tug on the back of your shoulder, plus the foot speed and the agility.

The big thing was what I learned from my roommate Gale Gillingham. Gale said, "Bill, right out of your stance you've got to punch him in the chest, then get your hands back in." So, basically, you had to try to create separation. If he was anywhere near you, his hands are like vise grips. I imagine that he could snap pliers all day long. I mean, this guy had a grip. I used to have bruises on the back of my shoulder where he would grab me.

Usually a guy can be real strong, but maybe not so quick on his feet. But then you get a guy like Bob who has both. And that guy had an engine and he never got into that idle mode. There were a lot of sleepless nights before those games.

## Len Hauss

### Center

*Team: Washington Redskins, 1964–77*
*His View: Hauss had to contend with Lilly flying between him and the guard for most of his career. After a while, he figured out his best chance of slowing Lilly.*

▌HATE TO SAY I did a lot of cut-blocking, but I did. It was legal in those days, and that was how you had to block. In my day, everybody cut-blocked. Whether he's coming inside or going straight over the guard, when you cut-block him, it would not be unusual to see his legs go up in the air. Picture yourself running straight at somebody and they hit you in the knees. If they knew how to cut-block, they'd flip you.

There was not much of a likelihood that you were going to win the battle if you hit Lilly in the shoulders or the chest, like you might try to block a guy one-on-one. He would throw you out of the way, run around you, or go through you.

He was going to beat you some, and if you were lucky you'd get him blocked a few times. But he was going to beat you more times than you were going to block him.

He's what you would draw up if you were drawing up a defensive lineman in the NFL. That's the first thing you think: "This guy is everything; what can I do to counteract what he does?"

# Larry Gagner

## Guard

*Teams:* *Pittsburgh Steelers, 1966–69; Kansas City Chiefs, 1972*
*His View:* *Gagner played for the Steelers long before they were Super Bowl–ready. Sacks weren't yet an official statistic, but Lilly set what was considered a team record with five in one game against Gagner in 1966.*

U NFORTUNATELY, I WASN'T a Christian at the time, or I'd have done a whole lot more praying before I faced him. We watched game films and stuff like that to get ready for him, and you'd see him beating a lot of people. At that time, he was probably the quickest man to ever play on the defensive line.

He gave me a baptism I'd just as soon forget. It was a rude awakening, because you just don't have anybody like that in college. After a while I got a little better because I had some familiarity.

He was a very clean player. I really respected him. But I didn't look forward to playing against Bob Lilly. I don't know any guards who did.

# CHAPTER 2

# FACING THE DOOMSDAY
# LINEBACKERS

---

**Chuck Howley**
**Outside Linebacker (1961–73), No. 54**
**Dallas Cowboys Ring of Honor**

**Lee Roy Jordan**
**Middle Linebacker (1963–76), No. 55**
**Dallas Cowboys Ring of Honor**

**T**OM LANDRY'S FLEX defense required everyone to play a specific role. Linemen were expected to read "keys" to try to figure out what the offense was doing. As part of the Flex, some defensive linemen set up closer to the line and some set up a yard or so back. The defense was designed so that linebackers, chiefly the middle linebacker, were free to make plays. With Chuck Howley and Lee Roy Jordan, the Cowboys had a steady presence at linebacker almost from the very start.

Jordan was the perfect middle linebacker for Landry's defense. He was a born leader with a high football IQ, the perfect combination to make sure everyone was in the right place. He was an undersized but hard-nosed tackling machine who was difficult to remove from a hole. Jordan once recorded a team-record 21 tackles in a game and retired as the leading tackler in franchise history. He held that distinction for nearly 30 years, until Darren Woodson caught him. Jordan started 154 straight games from 1966 to 1976.

Howley was a great athlete and a big hitter. He was disciplined and rarely out of position, putting himself in the right spot to make big plays. He intercepted two passes and recovered a fumble against Baltimore in Super Bowl V to become the first defensive player and only losing player named MVP. The next season, he recovered a fumble and intercepted a pass in the Super Bowl win over Miami.

# Norm Bulaich

## Running Back

**Teams:** *Baltimore Colts, 1970–72; Philadelphia Eagles, 1973–74; Miami Dolphins, 1975–79*

**His View:** *Bulaich had a good view of the plays that made Howley a Super Bowl MVP. He was the intended target on both of Howley's interceptions, one from Johnny Unitas and one from Earl Morrall.*

I DON'T RECALL THE details exactly, but on that first interception it was probably my fault. I was just a rookie and wasn't a good receiver. Maybe I cut the route off too soon or didn't go far enough, so I take all the blame because I was a rookie and stupid.

On that corner route that Earl threw in the end zone, it was about the same. Whether he underthrew me or whatever, I recall Howley just kind of came underneath and jumped the pass. Chuck was a better receiver than I was that day. The only good thing about it was I got to tackle Chuck.

Chuck was very keyed in to me that day. Chuck probably weighed 240 and he had speed. I remember him keeping up with me on pass patterns. Most linebackers couldn't do that in college, and it was like, "Welcome to the NFL."

I respected Chuck and Lee Roy and that whole defense that day. But I got a ring. They don't think I deserved it, but I got one. I always tell people that Chuck Howley still wears my number on his forehead. He was basically everywhere that day. Lee Roy was too. I remember Lee Roy hitting me head-on. He could deliver a blow.

# Charley Taylor

## Hall of Fame Wide Receiver

*Team: Washington Redskins, 1964–77*
*His View: At 6-foot-3 and 210 pounds, Taylor would be a big, strong receiver by today's standards. He was used as a running back too, meaning he faced Howley and Jordan while running, receiving, and blocking.*

**C**HUCK WAS MY guy. I had to crack block on him, and that was one of my favorite things to do. Chuck would get hung up on me. He was tough.

At the end of the day, they were the best, strongest, put-you-in-the-hospital team we would face. And Chuck was a big part of that, and so was Lee Roy. They weren't a finesse team. Chuck would buck up on you. They would all buck up on you.

# Conrad Dobler

## Guard

*Teams: St. Louis Cardinals, 1972–77; New Orleans Saints, 1978–79; Buffalo Bills, 1980–81*
*His View: Dobler graced the cover of a 1977* Sports Illustrated *with the headline "Pro Football's Dirtiest Player." He doesn't quibble with stories about him biting, punching, and generally creating trouble. However, he says he wasn't the only biter around.*

**O**NE TIME I caught Lee Roy Jordan right under his chin. Man, I put him down on his back. He grabbed my wrist and bit my thumb. It probably would have hurt, too, but his top retainer came out and all he could do was gum it. I was a young man at that time. It was my first or second year in the league, and I was thinking, "Oh, I guess biting's OK."

You got to understand something: When I was playing against those guys, I was young and full of piss and vinegar. These were older guys, and I'm just trying to make the team and stuff like that, so I'm not taking any prisoners. I'm going to eat their young.

I might have gotten into it with Lee Roy one time. He got hurt and he was kind of giving me the, uh, well, let's put it this way: There weren't a whole lot of five- or six-letter words coming out of his mouth. They were all four-letter words. Lee Roy, he probably doesn't like me so much.

Their linebackers used to make a lot of tackles in the backfield. Coach Don Coryell found a way to beat the Flex defense. What we did was, when we ran to the outside, we'd all just kind of go right down the line and close off all the gaps. That's kind of when Lee Roy got banged up a little bit, because he couldn't get through.

We wouldn't come off the ball; we'd just sort of peel off the line of scrimmage, and there were no gaps left. We were using terrible technique. We were so used to coming off the ball and knocking people off the ball, but here we were just kind of lining up and making a wall. We were all on each other's hip, kind of like a little train going down the line, so they couldn't slip through the gaps.

When the coaches came up with it we looked at them and said, "Come on, you can't be serious about us doing this." But it worked. Just imagine five offensive linemen putting their hands on each other's asses and going sideways.

# Mick Tingelhoff

## Hall of Fame Center

**Team:** *Minnesota Vikings, 1962–78*
**His View:** *Whenever the Vikings and Cowboys played, it was a battle of Iron Men in the middle. Tingelhoff never missed a game in his 17-year career, and Jordan never missed a game in his 11 years starting at middle linebacker.*

**H**E WAS FAST and very quick, and difficult to block. He knew how to read the offense. He moved quick, and he was hard to get to. Lee Roy was tough because he was so strong. He wasn't very big, but he always kept coming. He was really relentless.

We had some great battles with Dallas over the years, and I played him every single time. He was just a really good player and he was really smart, too. They were a really good team, and it was really tough when we played them.

# Len Hauss

## Center

**Team:** *Washington Redskins, 1964–77*
**His View:** *It's tough to top the rivalry between Hauss and Jordan. Not only did they face each other 27 times as part of the Washington-Dallas rivalry, they also squared off as college rivals, when Hauss was at Auburn and Jordan was at Alabama.*

**I**HAD THE MISFORTUNE of playing against Lee Roy. What stands out in my mind about Lee Roy is his speed and quickness. You better not miss getting to him. If you're going to block him, you better get in his face and stay in his face, because if he gets a step on you, he's going to make the play.

I'm thinking he weighed closer to 220, but if he weighed 210, it was 210 pounds of pure muscle that was pretty tough to block. He was one of the toughest I played against. He stood in there and took you on. Running most anything straight ahead or even a sweep, I've got to block Lee Roy, and one of the things I would do is fire out and cut him.

When you block a guy who was as quick as Lee Roy, then you better get to him and get him on the ground or he's going to get up and make the play. And it doesn't look good in film on Monday to see yourself standing behind Lee Roy and him making a tackle.

The last time I played against Lee Roy, I guess he knew he was getting out of the game. I blocked him and was able to knock him down and as we were getting up, Lee Roy says: "Good block, Len. Way to go." I think I must have jerked my head and just looked at him, and I'm thinking: "What's with this guy? We've knocked heads with each other hundreds of times and we've never said anything to each other."

# Jim Hart

## Quarterback

*Teams: St. Louis Cardinals, 1966–83; Washington Redskins, 1984*
*His View: The Cowboys and Cardinals became divisional rivals when the NFC East was formed in 1970. A 38–0 upset of Dallas that year is one of Hart's favorite memories of facing Howley and Jordan.*

THAT WAS THE most vivid and exciting time of all. One play from that game I still have a picture of. It was Chuck Howley and Jethro

Pugh hitting me. It was a third down and the picture—it looks awful. I think Howley is hitting me low and Jethro is hitting me high. I am contorted and the ball has left my hands.

Back then, the hash marks were college hash marks, so you were closer to the sideline. I was pretty much out on my feet, or as I lay on the turf. I can remember the coaches and players telling me: "Get off the field! Get off the field!" They didn't want to take a timeout. So I did end up getting off the field. It wasn't that far to crawl off. That was an awful, awful feeling.

Howley was just so smart. He was a grizzled veteran at that time, and I was a young guy. Going against someone like that, and as smart as I knew he was, as well as the rest of the Cowboy defense, it was awesome really. Especially to be playing against them so well as a team.

After that game we had to pinch ourselves: "Did we really do that? The Dallas Cowboys?" And the irony is, they went on to the Super Bowl. They won all the rest of their games, so we must have pissed them off.

That is the only time I can remember being hit by Howley, but I witnessed many hits that he put on running backs or wide receivers. He wasn't the fastest linebacker, but he knew angles. He played with his head, and when he got close enough he had the brawn to put the hurt on somebody. He was a student of the game even back then, when that wasn't talked about that much. It seemed like he knew where you were going to go with the ball before you threw it.

There is a bad memory of another game when we were going in to score down in Dallas. We're inside the 20-yard line and moving. A pass was called to Terry Metcalf across the middle. I anticipated Lee Roy Jordan going deeper in his drop. And then I threw it, right in Lee Roy's breadbasket. I probably spewed some expletives like I'm usually not wont to do. I just couldn't believe I did that.

Lee Roy was perfect for their situation. He wasn't wide like a Dick Butkus, not tall like a Jack Lambert, but just smart. He always seemed to be in position to make a play when you didn't expect him to be where he was. He would go back in coverage, I thought, then we'd run a draw and there he is back in the hole. And I'd be thinking, "How'd he get back in that hole in that quick a time?"

# Jackie Smith

## Hall of Fame Tight End

*Teams: St. Louis Cardinals, 1963–77; Dallas Cowboys, 1978*
*His View: Many fans remember Jackie Smith as the Cowboy who dropped a seemingly easy touchdown in the Super Bowl against the Steelers. But he broke into the league the same year as Jordan, and spent most of his 16 years battling Jordan and Howley as a Cardinal.*

**C**HUCK AND LEE Roy and all those linebackers were very disciplined players, so you knew when they lined up what their responsibility was going to be. But you still had to run the plays on them; you had to do it right. All of those guys could lay it on you.

Chuck did everything right. He was a tough guy to block. It was just kind of hard to get some good wood on him, especially because he knew the spot to be in. Chuck was always ready to anticipate what's going on.

Lee Roy was another one of those disciplined players who we had to really concentrate on. I would have to block on him quite a few times. If I ever got an inside release, I knew I was going to get hit by Lee Roy. So the deal was to try to avoid him, but I knew he was coming a lot of the time.

# Bill Curry

## Center

*Teams:* Green Bay Packers, 1965–66; Baltimore Colts, 1967–72; Houston Oilers, 1973; Los Angeles Rams, 1974

*His View:* At 235 pounds, Curry was not a large offensive lineman, so he understands the strategies Jordan used to dominate his opponents as an undersized linebacker.

**H**E WAS NEVER out of a play. He had this incredible grit and determination. The design of the defense was totally a gap control thing, and whichever gap he had, it was almost impossible to move him out of it.

He wasn't as big as the other middle linebackers, but he was the toughest guy to drive out of a hole because he had such great leverage. Once the direction of the play was established, he was one of the first ones there, if not the first.

There are always undersized players playing in the National Football League. There are a lot of undersized players in the league today. Heck, I was an undersized lineman. Undersized doesn't mean you can't play.

For Lee Roy, it was all about leverage. He could get under your pads and you couldn't get under his, and you weren't going to move him from his gap. Then he could get off that block and run. Usually if you're undersized, you can run faster than big guys. So us little guys, we have quickness, agility, and quick feet. He was tough as nails, too, I'll tell you that.

There weren't any slouches on that defense, not one, so you're going to get the same kind of comments about all of them: They were tough, they were disciplined, and they had great gap control.

# Billy Kilmer

## Quarterback

**Teams:** *San Francisco 49ers, 1961–66; New Orleans Saints, 1967–70; Washington Redskins, 1971–78*

**His View:** *There's no shortage of wild finishes and dramatic back-and-forth games in the Redskins-Cowboys rivalry. Jordan sniffed out Kilmer's plan in one of them, but still left Washington angry that day.*

IN 1975, WE were playing the Cowboys in Washington and I threw four interceptions. The last one, in the fourth quarter, I threw it to Cliff Harris and he ran it in for the go-ahead touchdown. The crowd was booing the hell out of me. But the score was still pretty close because I'd already thrown two touchdown passes.

There were about two minutes left in the game and we got the ball back. And we went right down the field and I threw a touchdown pass to Jerry Smith to tie the score. So we went into overtime. They got the kickoff and Roger Staubach right away threw an interception.

We got the ball and we're driving. I got in the huddle and said, "Listen, we're going to throw a touchdown." We'd already missed three field goals. I called a play action pass and hit Charley Taylor inside the 10-yard line. I gave it to Larry Brown and he got it inside the 1-yard line, then I called a quarterback sneak and jumped over and we won.

On that play Lee Roy Jordan was going to cover the fullback, and then he stepped over to the middle. He looked at me before the snap. I jumped over the line and he hit me right square in the jaw. He just came from nowhere and he kind of knew I might be doing that. When I just got it over the line, he hit me right square in the head. I'll never forget that. He was pissed.

# Harold Jackson

## Wide Receiver

*Teams:* Los Angeles Rams, 1968, 1973–77; Philadelphia Eagles, 1969–72; New England Patriots, 1978–81; Minnesota Vikings, 1982; Seattle Seahawks, 1983

*His View:* As a speedy outside receiver, Jackson didn't have to deal with Jordan very often. But he was well aware of him on September 26, 1971, when Jordan racked up a team-record 21 tackles.

**H**E WAS JUST a phenomenal football player, especially that day. Everybody tends to have that one good ball game, or two or three ball games in their career. And that was one career ball game for Lee Roy Jordan.

I don't know if they were having him line up and just freelance and roam all over the place. Most times they had their schemes and everything, but it just seemed like he was just roaming the field that day. He was all over.

# Ken Bowman

## Center

*Team:* Green Bay Packers, 1964–73

*His View:* Bowman is best known as the center who double-teamed Jethro Pugh, along with Jerry Kramer, for the game-winning score in the Ice Bowl. In most games against Dallas, he spent his time trying to track down Jordan and keep him out of the play.

**T**HE THEORY WAS, if you control the middle linebacker, you could control the defense. Control Lee Roy Jordan, and you could control the defense. From the center's standpoint, you had to be a jack-rabbit, because you had to get out on that middle linebacker. You had to be able to get on him before he decided to fill the hole. He was a tough guy to get to, and at times I knew the chances of getting to him before he got to the hole were pretty slim.

Dick Butkus was about 255 and a brawler, and he loved to tangle it up with you. Lee Roy would just as soon not see you for 60 minutes. He wanted to be someplace else, in the hole tackling the back. He wouldn't be as punishing as somebody like Butkus, but he was effective because he was so quick. He got out of there. He was pretty slippery.

## Tom Banks

### Center/Guard

*Team:* St. Louis Cardinals, 1971–80
*His View:* The Cardinals' powerful offensive line of the 1970s prided itself on aggressive, physical play. Against the Cowboys, Banks focused on trying to take Jordan down.

**W**E NEVER LOOKED at the whole situation as playing the great Cowboys teams. It was just another game to us. Our whole offense was just very physical and the Cowboys were a finesse defense. Whether anybody wants to admit it or not, it was just true.

We were able to put blockers on their linebackers so they couldn't run free, and it gave us a little more of an advantage. I would go out and chop, then we would shift the ball and sprint to the sideline. Then as Lee Roy was getting up after I knocked him down, I'd try to take his head off.

Lee Roy was great at going down and just coming right back up and flowing to the ball and making the play. If I could get to him, I was going to block him. The issue always was: Could we work out a way so I could get to him?

Lee Roy said I used to hold him. I'm blocking him and I'm blocking him and I'm blocking him. He's pissed off because I'm blocking him like I'm supposed to, and he starts screaming that I'm holding him.

I went to Auburn and he was an Alabama guy—and here in this state that holds a lot of weight. I said, "Lee Roy, the first time I got to hold you to block you is the day I quit this game." He was mad. He didn't speak to me for a long time after that.

The game has changed because of the size of the players, but still I don't know of anybody today who plays the game like Lee Roy did. I always admired the way he played the game.

## Tom Nowatzke

### Running Back

*Teams:* Detroit Lions, 1965–69; Baltimore Colts, 1970–72
*His View:* In Super Bowl V, a game remembered for hard-hitting defense and bumbling offense, Nowatzke took a pounding while providing a relative flurry of offensive output with 78 total yards and the fourth-quarter touchdown that tied the score.

THEY WERE AHEAD 13–6 at the half. And it was still 13–6 with about eight minutes to go. Where was the game played? Between the 40s. I tell you, it was the hardest-hitting game I ever played in.

Chuck and Lee Roy and all those linebackers were so good. They were tough. They didn't get out of position very often. It was just line up and hit as hard as you can. Believe me, it was the toughest game I ever played in, and I played 17 years of football.

We said at halftime that the first time we were in short yardage we were going to go weak side, which meant I carried the ball and Norm Bulaich blocked away from the tight end. Well, the first time was when we had it on the 3-yard line. They called the play and I run right up the back of the tight end. So we get back in the huddle and I told Earl Morrall, in some very colorful language: "I really messed up. Run the thing again and I'll get you a touchdown." And he did. I always kidded him for years that I had to call the play for him.

And then Dallas got the ball back and we intercepted again and kicked the field goal with nine seconds left to win it. That's how it happened. I remember when it was over Lilly was so mad he threw his helmet 100 feet into the air.

## Jerry Sisemore

### Offensive Lineman

*Team: Philadelphia Eagles, 1973–84*
*His View: By the time Sisemore came into the league, Jordan was in his 11th season. Sisemore thought the old man would be on the downside.*

IT'S AMAZING WHEN you grow up watching those guys on TV, and all of a sudden there they are. You'd think he'd get old and slow, since he'd been in the league forever. You'd think he'd slow down, but no, he got better and better.

With that defense, Lee Roy was absolutely perfect. The directing, and calling plays, and getting into the right place at the right time. You needed a middle linebacker in those days who ran the whole show. Lee Roy was that guy.

You couldn't run at him; half the time you couldn't run away from him. Now that it's over and I don't have to worry about them, I can say Lee Roy and all the rest of them were a classy bunch of guys. When we played them, we'd tell them they were bums—"Yous guys are bums!"

# CHAPTER 3
# FACING MEL RENFRO

**Defensive Back (1964–77), No. 20**
**Pro Football Hall of Fame, Dallas Cowboys Ring of Honor**

**MEL RENFRO BROUGHT** a mix of speed, athleticism, durability, and toughness to the rapidly improving Dallas defense. A star at running back and also at track at Oregon, Renfro started at safety right away with the Cowboys. He had seven interceptions as a rookie and led the league in kickoff and punt return average. Renfro was such a good athlete that he played safety, then moved to cornerback—the opposite of the usual evolution that sends aging corners to safety. Renfro was usually in the right position, and if he wasn't he had the speed to recover and make a play. He intercepted 52 passes and returned them for 626 yards, both team records. He returned three picks for touchdowns, including a 90-yarder. Renfro returned two kickoffs for touchdowns, including one for 100 yards, and still holds the team record for kick-return average (26.4 yards).

# Paul Warfield

## Hall of Fame Wide Receiver

*Teams:* Cleveland Browns, 1964–69, 1976–77; Miami Dolphins, 1970–74

*His View:* Warfield came into the league the same year Renfro did, facing him twice a year as a divisional rival and then later as a Super Bowl opponent. His surprising first glimpse of Renfro on a football field came before any of that, though.

I PLAYED AGAINST MEL when he was a member of the University of Oregon football team and I was at Ohio State. In preparation for that game, Woody Hayes, the legendary Ohio State coach, really set the tempo in telling us just how talented Mel was. He raved about the number of things he could do as a running back.

He also played defense. But he was a phenomenal running back who had tremendous breakaway speed and was a threat to go the distance whenever he touched the ball, whatever location he was on the field. I mean, he was a legitimate threat. I also played both ways. I played running back in the old T-formation setup that Ohio State employed, and I played defensive back.

While Woody Hayes had warned us of Mel's abilities and talents, it certainly registered with me once the ball game started. I recall a play when I started going to the right on a sweep. As I turned the corner and looked down the field, there was absolutely no one in sight. And so I'm kind of having a conversation with myself, that this is where I'll turn the dial and push the lever and go to light speed and this'll be over with. So I do that, and I go to light speed, and it's like slow motion.

Suddenly, I look over my shoulder and somebody's running right alongside me. I'm having this conversation with myself, and I'm noticing this guy running alongside me, and it's Mel Renfro. I'm saying to myself: "What are *you* doing here? No one has ever been here before. This is impossible that you are here because I'm at light speed." He pulled me down, and I did not go the distance for the touchdown. And during the course of the ball game, I reciprocated on him a couple of times, so we pretty much called it a draw.

That was my introduction to Mel Renfro on the football field. For the very first time on a football field, I had met someone who could do all the things that I could do . . . speed, athleticism, or whatever.

In my sophomore year, I went to the national track and field championships in Eugene, Oregon, and that's truly the first time I competed against Mel. We both were long jumpers, and Mel ran hurdles and I did a few other events. We both were in the finals of the long jump, and it was quite a duel. The interesting thing about it was that one inch separated the three top places. The winner was a track and field guy who was not a football player.

I have great respect for Mel Renfro because he's such a talented athlete, marvelously gifted. He simply was one of the most talented players I've ever faced, as a cornerback and a defenseman. And I really had such respect because he was a great, great sportsman also. You can have competitive rivalries and athletes can have great respect for one another's capabilities, and I think it was mutual.

I don't want to sound egotistical, but it was very difficult to match things that I could do in executing pass patterns and be able to react to me at the last second. And so if I fooled him on a pattern, and let's say for example a move to the inside on a play designed for me to go outside, then the quarterback could anticipate and throw the ball at just the right time. But even if I did momentarily fool him, Mel Renfro had the ability to recover and either intercept, or at the very least, deflect the ball.

So I had to work much harder to achieve or accomplish anything against Mel than I did against the vast majority of other defensive backs. And even though we had this ingenious scheme of route execution, he had these physical skills that made me work harder.

On every play he gave me everything he had, which I would have to say was more than I would get anywhere else. And I tried to do the same thing to him. Competing against Mel Renfro was a great, great challenge. As I learned at Ohio State, he was the one individual on the corner who could match me, skill for skill, ability for ability.

In the Super Bowl, the Dallas Cowboys were a better team than the Miami Dolphins at that juncture. When I went to Miami, the Dolphins were like an expansion team, and right about that period the Dallas Cowboys had come of age. Tom Landry came up with a scheme to nullify whatever effectiveness we thought I could have.

At that point, Cornell Green had shifted to strong safety. Both Mel Renfro and Cornell Green did a phenomenal job. I thought I could figure out what they were doing, but we were too young of a football team to make an adjustment to have any success.

We were trying to do some things that would get me in one-on-one coverage. There were some creative things going on, but whatever we proposed certainly did not work. We did some things, as I recollect, with me taking some different alignments, going into motion.

We were outclassed, outcoached, beaten thoroughly, and I think it dawned on our football team at the end of the game what it takes to win a title. That game did motivate us for our undefeated season the next year. Of course, the Dallas Cowboys were eliminated in the NFC Championship that next year and we faced the Redskins in that Super Bowl. But we were hoping for another shot at the Cowboys.

# Charley Taylor
## Hall of Fame Wide Receiver

*Team: Washington Redskins, 1964–77*

*His View: Taylor also was drafted the same year as Renfro and retired the same year. By the time they were done, Taylor had faced Renfro's Cowboys 22 times.*

**M**EL WAS THE quietest runner I ever faced. Normally you can hear a guy coming up on you. Mel would get up on you before you realized it. Next thing you knew, he was there. He was light on his feet. And he was so fast.

He would follow me all over the field. The three toughest guys for me were Lem Barney in Detroit, Charlie Waters, and Mel. They were so fast and so quick.

One time against Mel and Charlie, I was running a 15-yard crossing pattern, and the three of us got to the ball at the same time. The Dallas guys knocked each other back and there I was, still standing. Mel, he jumped over, because he never fell, and I beat him for a 40-something-yard touchdown.

But they would shut me down sometimes, with all of them working together. It was really great to play against those guys, because they brought out your best.

# Jim Hart

## Quarterback

*Teams: St. Louis Cardinals, 1966–83; Washington Redskins, 1984*
*His View: Hart loved throwing deep to receiver Mel Gray, who had a lot of big games against Dallas. His secret? Keeping his Mel away from their Mel.*

**I**'M SURE MEL Gray did beat him, but it seemed more like our right side—their left side—where Mel Gray had the most success. We really tried to throw away from Renfro.

If you couldn't get the throw on time, don't throw at him because he'll make up the ground and mess up the play, or at the worst intercept it. He had some real closing power. He could make you think like you had beaten him, then by the time you threw the ball he'd closed the gap and made it a toss-up when the ball got there.

Mel was steady. He was good for a long time; that was the great thing about him. He had staying power. He was somebody to reckon with all of his career.

# Harold Jackson

## Wide Receiver

*Teams: Los Angeles Rams, 1968, 1973–77; Philadelphia Eagles, 1969–72; New England Patriots, 1978–81; Minnesota Vikings, 1982; Seattle Seahawks, 1983*
*His View: Jackson remembers Renfro for his power as well as his speed.*

**M**EL WAS A real physical corner. He'd come up and bump and run and then run with you all over the field. He'd hit you all the way down the field. We kind of stayed away from Mel.

Mel was kind of a quiet corner over there. He was just a clean corner out there. The Cowboys would give you a lot of man coverage. They would depend on that front four they had and those linebackers.

# Billy Kilmer

## Quarterback

*Teams: San Francisco 49ers, 1961–66; New Orleans Saints, 1967–70; Washington Redskins, 1971–78*

*His View: As was the common practice of the day, Kilmer tried to avoid Renfro, unless he could get the much larger Charley Taylor on him. Even then, he knew it was risky.*

**M**EL WAS SO quick and he could cover most receivers man for man. He never needed any help, and I don't care what receiver was over there. You never threw over there when he was a corner, but it was pretty tough when he was taking away half the field.

So sometimes I'd go left formation and Charley Taylor would be over there and I would throw certain patterns that we knew Charley could run better. Charley was very fast in his prime, but Mel could stay right with him.

I also played against him when he was a safety. He was dangerous in both spots, the way he'd play the ball. He was one of the best free safeties I played against; then when they moved him to corner he could really cover.

# CHAPTER 4

# FACING BOB HAYES

---

**Wide Receiver (1965–74), No. 22**
**Pro Football Hall of Fame, Dallas Cowboys Ring of Honor**

**B**OB HAYES CAME to the Cowboys already known as the "World's Fastest Human," having won a pair of Olympic gold medals the previous year. No one had ever brought such speed to a football field, and "Bullet Bob" was a weapon from the start. As a rookie, he went over 1,000 yards with 12 touchdowns. Hayes is considered among the handful of players who revolutionized the game, as defenses were forced to adapt to his blazing speed. Hayes still holds the Dallas record with 71 receiving touchdowns—many of them dazzling. Nearly half went for 40 yards or more, including a team-record 95-yarder and catches of 89, 85, 82, 80, 76, and 74 yards. His career average of 20 yards per catch is still a Dallas record. Only Emmitt Smith (a Florida native like Hayes who followed him into jersey No. 22) and Tony Dorsett scored more touchdowns for the Cowboys.

# Ken Houston

## Hall of Fame Safety

*Teams:* Houston Oilers, 1967–72; Washington Redskins, 1973–80
*His View:* Houston remembers Hayes flying past defenders deep downfield whenever he wanted. Houston got his first dose of Hayes before becoming his division rival. When Houston was with the Houston Oilers, Hayes went for 187 yards and four touchdowns in one game.

**I**T WAS FRIGHTENING, really, because here's a guy who was a sprinter in a football player's body. He had blinding speed. But he wasn't on his toes. He ran more like a horse than a gazelle. You could just see him eating up ground when he came down. You knew that once he was within five yards, he was by you, basically.

The reason he was a Hall of Famer was because his speed changed the game completely. Back then, everybody ran a lot of man-to-man, and he could beat that on his own. You could bump and run off the line of scrimmage, but if you hit and missed, that was it. Teams had to go zone on him because guys were not half as fast as Bob Hayes. You had to do several things. They'd line up one guy on him and another guy deep.

The only real defense you had for him was to put a lot of pressure on the quarterback and hope that he didn't have enough time to throw it deep. A lot of times he would just be gone. Then he just kind of trotted back to the huddle. We'd laugh because we knew he had just outrun that quarterback's arm.

You had to be real physical with him and hope the wear and tear of the game would stop him. Being a strong safety, I'd mostly be on an outside zone. So my deal was to get out there and try to put my hands on him and slow him down. I never was caught up on him one-on-one. Sometimes I'd get him in the slot, but you always called out for help if you had him one-on-one.

Word got around among defensive backs: How do you cover this guy? What do you do? We used to all laugh about him . . . and they *still* laugh about it because there was really no way to cover him.

He was a real great guy, a real nice guy. I remember that. You know, we'd go out and we'd try to take a shot on him, and he'd smile or something like that. Occasionally he would get angry, but I thought his temperament was really good. He wasn't physical, but he could have been. I remember him from college, in a track uniform. He was probably the only one I know of who was built like that.

People today talk about, "Well, people are much stronger and much faster" and I just kind of look at them and laugh. I say, "No, not really." We had to cover Bob Hayes, Homer Jones, Paul Warfield. They were legitimate track speed, 100-meter guys. And they were out there running in those old heavy shoes. There's no telling how fast Bob would be running today. But I guarantee you, he would be leading the crop.

We go to some Hall of Fame gatherings, and his name will come up when people talk about fast guys, about guys playing today. Guys would just kind of start laughing when his name would come up.

They'd say, "Yeah, we remember Bob Hayes," because he was one of a kind.

# Paul Krause

## Hall of Fame Safety

*Teams: Washington Redskins, 1964–67; Minnesota Vikings, 1968–79*
*His View: Krause vs. Hayes was a matchup of big-play specialists, as Krause had the most interceptions in NFL history. The Purple People Eaters defensive line could get to a quarterback quickly and Krause was famous*

*for playing extremely deep, but still the Vikings made sure they accounted for Hayes.*

**W**HEN I PLAYED him, I had a pretty good look against him since I was so deep. Covering him one-on-one, though, there was just no way because he could just run so much faster than everybody. My goodness, when you played against Bob Hayes, you knew he was going to use his speed on you. We would have to double up on him or hit him off the line of scrimmage and let the corner run with him a little bit and then one of the safeties would cover deep.

You go into a game and you try to set up the defense for the game. We didn't change the whole defense just because Bob Hayes was on the field. But you sure looked at him. You had to know where he was.

I have to give Bob Hayes credit. He would catch the ball across the middle sometimes, but he was mostly an outside receiver. The smaller fast guys, they didn't like to go across the middle, because those linebackers would take their heads off.

I have a picture hanging up on the wall of a time I had knocked the ball away from him. He was just going to catch it and my hand was there and I had just gotten in front of the ball and knocked it down.

# Roger Wehrli
## Hall of Fame Cornerback

**Team:** *St. Louis Cardinals, 1969–82*
**His View:** *Wehrli had some success in slowing down Hayes, using the same basic approach every time.*

You always had to be ready to go deep with him. There was no secret about that. You could just not let your mind wander at all. Any time he was on my side, my thought pattern was: "He's going to go deep this play, so be ready. Don't let him close the cushion."

Obviously he was a good receiver, but not usually a receiver who was going to go over the middle or make a lot of moves on you. He was going to try to go deep on you at least two or three times a game. He was able to spread the defenses with the zone defenses and things like that. You had somebody who could really expand the field.

## Paul Warfield

## Hall of Fame Wide Receiver

*Teams: Cleveland Browns, 1964–69, 1976–77; Miami Dolphins, 1970–74*
*His View: Warfield was Hayes's teammate on the US track and field team, and, as a fellow member of the fraternity of pro football player/track stars, he admired Hayes's ability to fly down the field.*

**W**HILE I HAD great speed, Bob Hayes was the fastest human in the world. It was almost like there were those of us who had a level of speed considered great speed, and then Bob could run away from anyone.

The scheme that defensemen played against fast receivers was, as coaches would say, be deep as the deepest. So if you're going to keep Bob Hayes from catching the ball, you play off him and once the play starts you just take off and start running deep. You could never catch up to him to get beyond him. He could outrun the defensive coverage scheme even if it was a deeper defense. So it was never safe. And if he caught a ball between defenders, they would never catch him either.

I don't know if the game has seen that kind of speed since he came in. Yes, you can find guys who allegedly run a 4.2 40 over in Indianapolis now. I don't know, maybe Bob Hayes could run 3.9.

# Steve Preece

## Defensive Back

*Teams:* *New Orleans Saints, 1969; Philadelphia Eagles, 1970–72; Denver Broncos, 1972; Los Angeles Rams, 1973–76; Seattle Seahawks, 1977*
*His View:* *Preece recalls the dread of knowing that disaster and embarrassment were just a play away any time he lined up against Hayes.*

**B**OB HAYES, HE just put the fear of God in you. He was so much faster than I was, or practically anybody was, that you couldn't play him the same way. You just had to hit him. In the old days you could hit people downfield. But, if you got close enough to use your body on him, you were in trouble. He'd just run right by you. He'd take off and run the deep one.

When I covered him we'd have a lot of combination coverage, where the corner would hit Hayes and then the free safety would rotate to that side and have him. So as a safety I'd be coming from a distance. I'd be trying to play nothing but angles. And you're hoping, your only prayer is, that he'd get a good bump from the corner or a linebacker so you can get your body in a position to cut the guy off. It was difficult.

Bob was a good pattern runner, but he didn't have to be as good because you were so afraid of him going deep. He always had a very large cushion to get open on the short stuff. He would run a lot of takeoffs. About four or five times a game, he just ran straight down the field and that was the pattern. They threw it to him, and he'd catch a couple of them.

You'd have him coming across the middle and you just looked for an opportunity to hit him. That's what coaches would encourage against Bob Hayes—just hit the guy as much as you could to try to slow him down. He was tough. I'm sure Bob took more hits than many because with his speed that was the only way you could try to discourage him.

You always worried about hurting your team with a big play and getting smoked for a touchdown. He scared you to death. You didn't worry about anything with Bob Hayes except getting totally embarrassed.

## Ken Bowman

### Center

*Team: Green Bay Packers, 1964–73*
*His View: Hayes's speed had impact where you might not expect it—like the Packers' pregame meal before the 1966 NFL Championship game.*

**B**ACK THEN YOU had a steak for your pregame meal. I was with our cornerback Herb Adderley, and Herb barely touched his steak. I said, "Herb, give me your steak if you're not going to eat it. I'll eat it."

He said, "Well Bow, I've got to try to stay with the World's Fastest Human." It made such an impression on me that I pushed my plate away and I didn't even eat my steak that night. If Herb wasn't going to eat it, I wasn't going to either.

# CHAPTER 5

# FACING RAYFIELD WRIGHT

Tackle (1967–79), No. 70
Pro Football Hall of Fame, Cowboys Ring of Honor

NICKNAMED "BIG CAT," Rayfield Wright was the perfect player to protect franchise quarterback Roger Staubach. He was a big, strong, steady presence who almost always used perfect technique every play. Wright was incredibly athletic; he played basketball and football in college, and the Cowboys tried him at tight end and defensive end before he took over at right tackle. He manned that spot so well that he was selected to the NFL's All-Decade Team for the 1970s. Right tackle was the pivotal spot on the offensive line back then because so many great pass-rushers came from that side. In fact, when Wright got his first start—as an injury replacement in 1969—the first defensive end he faced was future Hall of Famer Deacon Jones of the Rams' Fearsome Foursome. He did so well that he went into the following training camp as the starter.

# Jack Youngblood

## Hall of Fame Defensive End

*Team:* Los Angeles Rams, 1971–84
*His View:* Youngblood always braced for tough battles against Wright, particularly after he famously broke his leg against Dallas in the 1979 playoffs at Texas Stadium.

**F**ACING RAYFIELD WAS both a nightmare and a privilege. We would compete as hard as you can on the field, and then off the field, he was just one of the best human beings you ever want to be around. On the field, he was ugly, though. He was ugly to me.

Rayfield was so talented. It was technique and athleticism that made him difficult. He was strong, but he just always had himself in position to play, and to play well. I tried my best to stay as far away from him as possible. I tried my best to use speed and quickness. He had body position because he had such great feet. He knew where his cutoff point was, and he could get there and cut you off most of the time.

You knew that, at best, you were going to best him once or twice a ball game and make that sack. Rayfield never had a scowl on his face. He was always smiling. We'd come to a draw, and he would still have a smile on his face.

I remember when I broke my leg, he came over right there at first, when I was rolling around on the ground like a turtle. It was a very quick, "You OK?" And I gave a little thumbs-up or something, because you don't want to admit that you're on the deathbed.

Then I'm in the locker room getting it taped up and I'm thinking: "I've got a hard enough time against him on two good legs. Now I'm really in trouble." I'm thinking this is going to basically be impossible. You just have to grit your teeth sometimes and try to go and play and compete.

After I came back, Rayfield was just as bad to play against as he'd ever been. There is no mercy in that 60 minutes. The pain was excruciating;

it really was. Every time I took a step it felt like somebody was stabbing a knife into my fibula.

It takes away most of your movement to your right when you have to try to push off of that leg. There were times I remember that I tried to move. I'd do it just instinctively, because that's the move that's there, and the body fails. It hurt so bad I just went to the ground.

I'll always remember Rayfield coming over when I was down on the field and saying he hoped everything would be all right. When your opponent has a respect for you, it's very gratifying. You appreciate that, and you remember those guys who have that kind of character.

## Carl Eller

## Hall of Fame Defensive End

*Teams:* *Minnesota Vikings, 1964–78; Seattle Seahawks, 1979*
*His View:* *Wright always created problems for Eller. In their most famous battle, in the 1975 playoffs, Eller managed to get by Wright for three sacks. Wright, however, kept Eller clear of Roger Staubach on the game-winning Hail Mary pass.*

IN THE HAIL Mary game, I was actually very close to being able to make that sack. I was really in position. I don't remember all the other sacks, because Rayfield was very, very tough and not a player I would expect to have a great game against. I think perhaps I was more speedy with him that day, probably just getting out of his range.

Rayfield was an excellent tackle. He was tall, with excellent balance and a good arm reach. He would probably extend those long arms a little more than the rules allowed. He was quick and lean and had very good feet.

Rayfield was very careful and very calculated. He would get up and get back quickly. He wasn't one of the bigger tackles I played against strength-wise and weight-wise. But he was very active.

Tony Dorsett used to sneak behind Rayfield and those guys, and you really couldn't get to him. He'd really just kind of pick his way and choose his way. They would keep their guys tied up before he would break loose.

Rayfield wasn't loud or rowdy or talkative. But I wasn't either, so maybe that was sort of setting the stage for that. That was pretty consistent with Landry's teams. They were pretty disciplined guys.

He was very challenging, so when I did have good days against him, those were really feathers in my cap.

# Claude Humphrey

## Hall of Fame Defensive End

**Teams:** *Atlanta Falcons, 1968–78; Philadelphia Eagles, 1979–81*
**His View:** *The Falcons weren't very good for most of Humphrey's time there. Facing Wright and the star-studded Cowboys just seemed like rubbing it in.*

**WHEN YOU'RE ON** a losing team, you come into the game mad. I'm not one of the ones who consider them America's Team, but they were a great football team. As good as we'd play against them, the scoreboard would always say they won. That gave me more motivation when I played Dallas. Everybody on their team was an all-star.

Sometimes I got mad at Rayfield. Every time Rayfield blocked me, I thought he was holding me. Even though he wasn't, he was just doing his job like I was, it just appeared to me that way. But I don't ever remember getting in many fights with Rayfield.

There weren't a whole lot of tricks to Rayfield's game. He just went out there and beat you down. He was a no-nonsense player. He just got down to business. When he decided he was going to shut you out, that's exactly what he did.

It was hard to get him off balance, to pull him one way or the other. The first thing he would do was drop those big hands and arms on you. And then you were pretty well done for. He dropped those hands and arms wherever he could get them on you, but most of the time it was on your chest.

What he managed to do was stand you up and break your momentum. Then he'd have you, then he'd just run you right by the quarterback. Or if you were going the other way he'd just push you into the pile. What he really wanted to do was get his hands on your upper body.

In those days, unlike today, guys weren't so overweight that in the fourth quarter they couldn't play. Rayfield was just as good in the fourth quarter as he was in the first quarter. He was capable of doing his job, all day long.

I compare him to Ron Yary, Forrest Gregg, or Bob Brown. Back then if you faced one you faced them all. They were the really good athletes who didn't have any weaknesses.

# Clarence "Sweeny" Williams
## Defensive End

*Team:* *Green Bay Packers, 1970–77*

*His View: Dallas drafted Williams in 1969, and he spent a year on the Taxi Squad, a forerunner of the practice squad, before being traded to Green Bay. Though Williams only faced Wright a handful of times as a Packer, he saw him more times than he can count in practice.*

**H**E HELPED ME get my career started because he told me some things that I needed to work on, and things that he had difficulties with against defensive linemen. In those days, we could do things like head slap them and all that kind of stuff when they'd come off the ball. He said that that kind of hurt, especially when Deacon Jones would get him.

Rayfield told me, since I was so young, that I needed to watch every time a guy lines up. He told me that if an offensive lineman is doing something he's doing it for a reason. He might lean back or lean forward or set back on his hand. It's things like that. He taught me how to use my hands, how to grab an offensive lineman and get rid of him.

A couple times he knocked me on my behind, and then he told me what I was doing wrong and why he did that. Being young and not having experience, he told me lots of things to look out for. He was just a great guy. He took to me. Some of those veterans didn't, but he knew I wasn't a threat to take his job.

The first time I came up against him as a Packer, I was nervous. I was scared. I knew he was good. I had a good game against him; he didn't annihilate me. I think I got a sack or at least made Staubach throw early. I can't remember exactly, but I know I didn't get embarrassed.

*Extra Point*

# America's Team

Although the Dallas Cowboys were one of the most successful team of the 1970s, they weren't tagged as "America's Team" until *after* their fifth and final Super Bowl of the decade.

The name arrived in a rather unspectacular fashion, too, considering how iconic it's become: NFL Films Editor-in-Chief Bob Ryan dreamed it up for the team's highlight film of the 1978 season, which ended with a bitter 35–31 loss to the Pittsburgh Steelers.

"Looking through the footage there was something I had seen not just in 1978, but in the previous five years: There was no doubt that the Cowboys were the NFL's top team," Ryan said. "They were really interesting not only because they won, but they were like the Yankees, Notre Dame, and the Celtics. The Cowboys were in that group. You loved them or you hated them."

The evidence of greatness was all there on film, Ryan recalled. The Cowboys were on the national TV games on Sunday and on *Monday Night Football* more than other teams, and they always drew huge ratings. They had the cheerleaders, their own Spanish network, the computerized scouting, and the memorabilia.

"This was way before the NFL started marketing jerseys and hats and paraphernalia, but when you looked at the footage you saw people in Cowboys paraphernalia," Ryan said. "There were so many Staubach jerseys."

The star power didn't hurt either.

"That team had enough stars to make up a galaxy," Ryan said. "They had Staubach, Tony Dorsett, the Doomsday Defense. It was all there, so my hook was, I could put this all together in a film. But what do I call it? I thought of a bunch of things, and I called their PR man and I said, 'How about America's Team?' I told him about all the reasons and he loved it."

The phenomenon took off after the first home preseason game the next year, when the team was announced over the PA system as America's Team. Cowboys President and General Manager Tex Schramm loved it, and so did all the team's marketing people.

"The people who didn't like it were the coaches, especially Tom Landry," Ryan said. "There was enough hatred of the Cowboys to begin with, and this was just more fuel to the fire."

Cowboys coaches weren't alone in their dislike of the name.

When former Steelers great Joe Greene was told this book was named *Facing America's Team,* he said: "America's Team? . . . Oh, so you're writing about the Pittsburgh Steelers?"

Longtime Redskins quarterback Billy Kilmer also questioned whether the name was pinned on the wrong franchise.

"I went on a USO tour after our Super Bowl and lot of our servicemen loved the Redskins," he said. "And I always thought, because we were the nation's capital, because most of the military guys loved us, we were America's Team, really."

Other players felt robbed as well.

"The Minnesota Vikings could have been America's Team if Drew Pearson didn't push off on Nate Wright in the Hail Mary game," former Vikings running back Chuck Foreman said. "That was our best team. We would have won the Super Bowl."

Former Colts running back Tom Matte thought the moniker belonged in Baltimore, which after all beat the Cowboys in their first Super Bowl appearance of the 1970s and was a longtime NFL power.

"That always teed us off a little bit," he said. "We thought the Baltimore Colts were America's Team after we won two NFL Championships in 1958 and 1959."

Other players didn't necessarily want the label, but didn't like it, either.

"Our reaction to it was: Who cares? They weren't any more America's Team than we were. They had fun with it, so good for them," said Tom Mack, a Hall of Fame guard with the Rams.

"They wore those gray, Confederate-looking uniforms, and I always wondered: Why would they call them America's Team when they have Confederate uniforms?" former Cardinals lineman Conrad Dobler said.

"I still can't make my mouth say they are America's Team, but it is a fact," former Green Bay linebacker Na'il Diggs glumly acknowledged. "You can ask someone just coming into the country what they think of in America as far as sports goes, and they'll usually say the Dallas Cowboys. That's just the way it is."

# Section 2
# Roger's Team

THE COWBOYS BEGAN the 1970s by finally making it to the Super Bowl—the first of five in the decade. Their first Super Bowl featured Craig Morton at quarterback, and ended in heartbreaking defeat to the Baltimore Colts on a field goal in the final seconds. The Cowboys returned the very next season and won their first title with a three-touchdown victory over the Miami Dolphins. Roger Staubach was the game's MVP, further affirmation of Coach Tom Landry's mid-season decision to give him the starting job.

The Cowboys made it to three more Super Bowls in the decade, highlighted by their dominating victory over the Denver Broncos after the 1977 season. The Cowboys also lost twice to the Pittsburgh Steelers. In each of the games, which came after the 1975 and 1978 seasons, the Steelers built leads and then held off furious comeback charges by Staubach.

Even with those tight losses to the Steelers, the Cowboys' domination of the decade was impressive. They won seven NFC East titles, went to seven NFC Championships, and made the playoffs every year but one. They also became America's Team, the label they were given after the 1978 season that has stuck with them ever since, thanks in large part to the biggest stars of the era: Staubach, Cliff Harris, Charlie Waters, Drew Pearson, Randy White, Harvey Martin, Ed "Too Tall" Jones, and Tony Dorsett.

# CHAPTER 6

# FACING ROGER STAUBACH

Quarterback (1969–79), No. 12
Pro Football Hall of Fame, Dallas Cowboys Ring of Honor

**R**OGER STAUBACH WAS the undisputed leader of America's Team, respected and admired by fans and foes alike. He was the face of one of the greatest teams of the 1970s, winning two Super Bowls and a Super Bowl MVP, and performing heroically in a pair of very close Super Bowl losses. He was named to the NFL's All-Decade team of the 1970s, topping the likes of Bob Griese and Fran Tarkenton.

Staubach did it all after a very late start; he wasn't the full-time starter until he was nearly 30 years old, after serving in the Navy and then winning a drawn-out position battle. Staubach was known for scrambling, creating on the fly, fearlessness, and extreme competitiveness. He ranks third on the Dallas career passing yardage list, behind Tony Romo and Troy Aikman, but he was known mostly for *when* he produced statistics. He's the Cowboys career leader in postseason touchdown passes. He earned the Captain Comeback nickname while putting together 23 fourth-quarter comebacks (or, about one every six games he played).

# Jack Ham

## Hall of Fame Linebacker

*Team:* *Pittsburgh Steelers, 1971–82*
*His View:* *Twice in a four-year span in the 1970s, the famed Steel Curtain defense found itself fending off late rallies by Staubach during the Super Bowl. He was sacked 12 times in those two games, and hit many more times.*

**H**E TOOK A pretty good beating that second game and he was still firing that thing. I'm not sure if he doesn't get one more shot that they don't win the game, to tell you the truth. We hit him with everything we had. You talk about a quarterback on the tough side, but he was just one competitor that you nearly had to kill to beat. That's why I had so much respect for him.

We always felt Roger is one quarterback who's not going to quit on you. He's going to fight. And I think in those last series, that's when we got a lot of hits on him, because we're not taking play action with a big lead like that.

If we would have lost that game, I think half our team would have been headed to the bridge and jumping off, because we had control of the game. But you know, especially in Super Bowls, you never count that thing until the game is over.

After the game, I actually went in their locker room and he was in there being interviewed by reporters. I just wanted to tell him that I really respected him. We didn't play a quarterback who took that kind of beating and still got up and just kept fighting.

He was probably shocked that a Steeler was in his locker room, but I just wanted to tell him what a great game he played. The two best teams played and we were fortunate to come out on top.

# Carl Eller

## Hall of Fame Defensive End

*Teams: Minnesota Vikings, 1964–78; Seattle Seahawks, 1979*
*His View: Eller remembers chasing Staubach around, particularly in their 1975 playoff game. Eller sacked him three times that day, but missed him plenty, too, including on Staubach's 50-yard prayer to win the Hail Mary game.*

**I**DON'T KNOW HOW many times Roger escaped that day, but he would always slide away. He was very cagey that way. When he was bottled up, he would get out of there and get the first down. What made Roger tough was he got positive yards most of the time—he'd squirm out and just get the positive yards.

In the Hail Mary game, I thought we had it in the bag. If he would have held the ball any longer I would have made the sack, but he threw it up there. He threw it so vertical that I was thinking, "No way is it going to be complete."

Overall, when you're talking about Roger, I think he had a good grasp of what his own talents and abilities were and what he should do in certain situations. And he'd typically do it. He was very, very clever. I thought he was a good leader. I had a lot of respect for Roger. I always thought he was a very thoughtful, considerate player, very sportsman-like but also a very tough competitor.

# Joe Greene

## Hall of Fame Defensive Tackle

*Team: Pittsburgh Steelers, 1969–81*

*His View: Greene worried about Staubach's ability to make the most of broken plays when he faced him in the Super Bowl.*

**H**IS STRENGTH, WELL, among many, was how he would move in the pocket. But he could also break the line of scrimmage and move the ball down the field and get first downs. He could beat you with his feet, with his arm, with his ability to think. And all of that was driven with his high level of motivation and competitiveness.

At every position we had Pro Bowl–caliber players. That means when Roger dropped back to pass, he not only had good guys breathing down his neck, but he also had difficulty finding open receivers because of the talented linebackers and secondary.

In our second Super Bowl against the Cowboys, when they scored two touchdowns late in the game, it was Roger at his best. It was very hectic. Roger with the ball in his hands with four seconds on the clock, 10 seconds on the clock, 30 seconds on the clock, it's very precarious.

That's not a good feeling. They were that same way in our first Super Bowl. A touchdown would have won it for them. So regardless of what went on the first three quarters, they got real hectic at the end.

In the second game, I think I had a piece of Roger's leg and he got away from me, and he got away from several of us. He got a first down, and that was big to them because they were trying to make a comeback.

I had a tendency at times to talk with quarterbacks, but I never did get into a dialogue with Roger because Roger was too smart for that. He wasn't going to waste his time arguing with some defensive lineman because all I would give to him is trouble. If he was paying attention to me, he wasn't looking downfield.

I thought that athletically we were one of the few teams that could match up with the Cowboys across the board, offensively and defensively. You look at them and by position they were pretty well suited to deal with just about any team.

The games that the Steelers and the Cowboys had, to me as a fan, you want to see those kinds of matchups, because each team made the other better. And you know what? Everybody enjoyed it. Right up till the end, you didn't know who was going to win it.

## Ken Houston
### Hall of Fame Safety

*Teams: Houston Oilers, 1967–72; Washington Redskins, 1973–80*
*His View: Spending the whole game chasing Staubach brought out the worst in Houston and other Washington defenders.*

**WE WANTED TO** hit Roger so bad it was unbelievable. When he'd break out and run, we wanted to hit him and stop him and don't ever let him run again. When you finally got a chance to put lick on him, you'd just try to end his career. But he'd make those miraculous plays.

We worried about his legs. You'd pressure him, but he had a way of escaping. You never thought about him being fast. He didn't even look fast. He was like a Fran Tarkenton back then in those days. They'd get in that pocket for about a half a minute, then it was off to the races. You talk about original scramblers. I don't think you can talk about scramblers without talking about Staubach and Tarkenton.

We figured it out later on that you had to blitz him, because you had to get the ball out of his hands. If you let him keep the ball he was going to run around back there, he was going to find somebody, and it was going to be another spectacular play. We would make a go at him and get a lick in on him and try to at least make him get rid of the ball.

He had a great amount of physical and mental toughness. There was no question that Roger was the leader of that team. They had a lot of name players, a lot of great players, but you cannot be on a Dallas team without coming through Roger Staubach.

# Jack Youngblood
## Hall of Fame Defensive End

*Team: Los Angeles Rams, 1971–84*
*His View: Youngblood was a fierce pass-rusher who could get to Staubach. The problem was, he often couldn't grab hold of him after he got there.*

**H**E HAD THAT unique quality, almost like it was a sixth sense. He knew the pressure was coming, and he seemed to have a visual of where he could step around it or step behind it and escape. So you had to play real smart with Roger.

I missed Roger so many times because of his escapability. I had him dead to rights. He probably got out more than I got him. I have to admit that. I told him: "Do you have eyes in the back of your head? What in the world? How'd you know I was *right there?*"

He had both the physical and the intellectual aspect of playing the game. He knew what they wanted to do, knew what they had in the game plan, and had the ability to get the ball where it needed to be.

# Roger Wehrli
## Hall of Fame Cornerback

**Team:** *St. Louis Cardinals, 1969–82*
**His View:** *Wehrli intercepted Staubach more than any other quarter-back he faced in his career, six times in all. Half of them came in a 1975 showdown that helped the Cardinals lock up their second straight NFC East title.*

**WE JUST HAD** their number that night. That's one game that I remember best. I remember the good ones better than the bad ones. He was one of the best quarterbacks I faced, but I probably just had many more opportunities to intercept him because we played against each other so much.

I think what made Roger so good was that he was such an all-around athlete. I remember covering Pearson and those guys and just thinking we had made a good play. And then you look around and there's Roger scrambling around and our linemen can't catch him.

Obviously, I respected him. He was fun to play against, and certainly difficult to play against. The whole Dallas offense was ahead of its time.

We did well in the mid-70s against Dallas. Obviously they won a lot more than we did, but when Coach Coryell was here, for three or four years he had real good success against them. You knew if you were going to contend for a division championship, they were probably the team you had to go through.

# Joe Theismann
## Quarterback

**Teams:** *Washington Redskins, 1974–85*
**His View:** *Staubach was one of Theismann's heroes, but he also happened to play for his most hated rival.*

**I**N MY CAREER against the Cowboys, whether as a punt returner or the starting quarterback, whatever it was, they're the most vivid games in my mind. They're the characters within the game that I remember the most—and of course having a chance to play against Roger.

Roger was my idol. He was the one man I wanted to be compared to, because Roger went to the military service and then went on to the NFL. I spent three years in the Canadian Football League and then came back. Roger had his competition between he and Craig Morton, and mine was between Billy Kilmer, Sonny Jurgensen, and I. There were some similarities between our careers.

You have to appreciate and admire greatness. I'd be screaming "Get him!" and then I'd find myself saying, "Dang, he's good." And, "Darn he's lucky." I had the opportunity to compete against one of the greatest guys who ever played this game.

# Dick Anderson
## Safety

**Team:** *Miami Dolphins, 1968–77*
**His View:** *Anderson believes Staubach earned his Super Bowl MVP for more than his statistics against the Dolphins.*

**R**OGER'S NOT A quarterback to be feared. There were others like Johnny Unitas and Joe Namath you probably feared more than Roger, but Roger had an innate ability to lead a team. Roger had a great command of the game, and they were clicking. And you always had to be concerned because he was such a great athlete—he ran when he had to.

Their game plan was better than our defense. We were a very aggressive defense and pursued with a lot of vigor on the outside plays. They obviously saw that in their preparations, and Duane Thomas had a great game and he broke everything back to the center.

## Jeff Siemon

### Linebacker

**Team:** *Minnesota Vikings, 1972–82*
**His View:** *Staubach is known for being extremely competitive in everything he does. Siemon saw that trait on Sundays, and also once in a game that didn't seem to merit Staubach-like intensity.*

**B**Y THE TIME you get to the NFL most people are great competitors, but I think Roger was above and beyond even. He would have been in the top 5 percent of competitive players. You knew he was going to give everything he had.

He was fully engaged, he hated to lose, and he would do everything he could to win. That was the highest priority for him—within the rules. He was a wonderful person through and through. I have a lot of respect for him as a man and a person. He has high morals. When the chips were down you could count on him to make a valiant effort.

We did a weekend where we were involved in a Christian outreach to high schools and we played a little flag football game where fans could come and observe. How competitive was that game? What do you think? There was no difference. That's who he is. He's going to be competitive, whether it's his real estate company or in the Super Bowl, or playing in a pickup flag football game.

He was also a very smart, savvy quarterback. He wasn't going to make mental mistakes, and he was going to take advantage of opportunities the defense presented him. He was obviously a class act on top of it all. He's an easy guy to respect, and even root for, when you weren't playing against him.

# Steve Foley

## Defensive Back

*Teams:* Denver Broncos, 1976–86
*His View:* The Broncos knew they couldn't afford to keep turning the ball over to Staubach if they were to have a chance in Super Bowl XII.

**W**E HAD BEATEN the Oakland Raiders and the Steelers, who were in the midst of their four Super Bowls, so we knew we could play with Dallas. But we knew we had to have a really good game.

You just couldn't give the Dallas Cowboys' offense eight turnovers and expect to come out with a win. They're just too powerful; they're going to score if you give them that many tries because they had a lot of offensive weapons.

Roger was so hard to defend because if you had everybody covered, he could run around the pocket until somebody got free. They didn't call him Roger the Dodger for nothing. If you blitzed him and missed, well, everybody's running man-to-man so you might not get him for 10 or 15 yards. So that definitely caused some concern.

I remember early on that Roger handed the ball off to Tony Dorsett and it hit him in the chest plate and it bounced down the field, loose, and they recovered it, I believe for a first down, and you're just kind of shaking your head going, "Come on."

They had a punt they fumbled in the end zone, and we had five guys around it who could have recovered, and Aaron Kyle, who wound up playing with us later, recovered the fumble for them. And you're like, "I can't believe they got that ball back."

We were hanging in there the best we could, but again, you can't give Roger Staubach and all those weapons the ball that much and expect to hold them out.

# Chris Hanburger

## Hall of Fame Linebacker

*Team:* Washington Redskins, 1965–78
*His View:* Talk about opposites—Hanburger was an Army guy who played defense for Washington. Staubach was a Navy guy who played offense for Dallas.

**I WAS IN THE** Army right out of high school, then got out and went to college. I grew up in a military family, too. My father was a career Army officer. So my life growing up was very regimented, and I think my time in the service reinforced all of that, and that molded me to the person I am to this day. I think Roger was that way, too, from going through the Naval Academy and his military experience.

# Herm Edwards

## Cornerback

**Teams:** *Philadelphia Eagles, 1977–85; Atlanta Falcons, 1986; Los Angeles Rams, 1986*
**His View:** *As somebody who grew up a fan of the Cowboys, Edwards knew Staubach was dangerous. He saw it firsthand when he was starting in the Eagles' secondary as a rookie.*

YOU THINK ABOUT all those comebacks the Cowboys ended up winning, with Staubach's ability to bring his team back with his arm and with his legs as well. You did not want to play the Cowboys in two-minute defense.

You knew you had to get him in an uncomfortable third down, and therein lies the problem because Roger was good enough to where if things were covered he would extend things with his legs. He was a take-off-and-run guy, too. He didn't run like the other guys—he could go.

There's not a classier guy to play the position than Roger. There have been some great quarterbacks, but he was probably the best I've had to face. And I faced a lot of good quarterbacks. He was like Captain America because the Cowboys were the team to beat. He was a great guy, and he did it the right way.

I loved playing against those guys. The first year I played them, they came to Philly and beat us. It was cold. I can remember in the fourth quarter, they were taking a knee and stuff. Bill Bergey, our middle linebacker, he couldn't stand the Cowboys. So, the game was basically over, but Bergey kept calling timeouts because it was cold and he wanted to keep them out there.

Bergey said, "We may not win, but we're going to keep them out here in this cold as long as we can." I remember Roger looking over at the defense and obviously thinking, "What are you guys calling time-outs for?"

# Lemar Parrish

## Cornerback

*Teams:* Cincinnati Bengals, 1970–77; Washington Redskins, 1978–81; Buffalo Bills, 1982

*His View:* The last regular-season game of Staubach's career went about how you might expect: He led a furious comeback against the hated Redskins with the NFC East title on the line. Staubach's final regular-season pass went eight yards to Tony Hill in the end zone with just 39 seconds left, beating Parrish with a perfect pass for a 35–34 win and the last of his 23 career comeback victories.

**I WAS LOOKING FOR** an inside route on that last play because that's what they were usually looking for on me. I wasn't looking for an outside route. It was a perfect pass. I can remember as soon as Roger got the ball in his hand . . . and then Tony Hill made a great catch. Roger did what he had to do, being a great quarterback.

I remember quite well because I was having just a great game. I don't think anyone was throwing anything on my side. But then there was this one particular play. The offensive coordinator from the Cowboys told me later, "I knew every time we'd get close to that goal line, we were going to go to Tony down on the outside." I had a great year that year, but that one play down there hung over me.

It wasn't a good feeling because I'm a proud man and I don't ever want those kind of things to happen to me. What was going through my mind in that fourth quarter was just playing that receiver in front of me. I always had the idea that if the receiver can't beat me, the quarterback can't beat me either. But Roger was exceptional.

If the guy was open, Roger was going to hit him. He did a lot of great things, and he had some great receivers. Roger was magnificent. He was the best comeback man I've ever seen, the best in the business. It wasn't a good thing to want to face him if he was down by three or seven points because he could strike from anywhere.

Roger was a tough competitor, he was smart, he was accurate, he had all the attributes. If there was any time on the clock at all, he could beat you. Roger's one of the best there ever was, and he'd beat anybody if he got the time. I enjoyed playing against him because I liked to play against the best.

# CHAPTER 7
# FACING CLIFF AND CHARLIE

Cliff Harris
Safety (1970–79), No. 43
Dallas Cowboys Ring of Honor

Charlie Waters
Defensive Back (1970–81), No. 41

CLIFF HARRIS AND Charlie Waters patrolled the Dallas secondary throughout the 1970s, and they were often considered an indistinguishable unit. Opponents talked about Cliff and Charlie much more often than just Cliff or just Charlie. They were a hard-hitting duo that frustrated quarterbacks, made big plays, and fearlessly scrapped with anybody, even much larger offensive linemen. Harris made the Cowboys as an undrafted rookie out of tiny Ouachita Baptist in Oklahoma and won the free safety job as a rookie. Known as "Captain Crash" for his brutal hits, Harris was named to the NFL's All-Decade Team of the 1970s. Waters was drafted in the third round out of Clemson in 1970. He played a few years at cornerback before taking over at strong safety for good in 1975. Waters shares the NFL record with nine postseason interceptions, including three in a 1977 game against Chicago.

# Jim Hart

## Quarterback

*Teams: St. Louis Cardinals, 1966–83; Washington Redskins, 1984*
*His View: No quarterback faced Harris and Waters more than Hart. He was the Cardinals' starter before they got to Dallas and after they left. Hart faced Harris and Waters nearly 20 times, and the cagey safeties looked to fluster him every time.*

**O**NE TIME CLIFF is fooling around and I'm under center sort of waiting to start the cadence. I'm standing there thinking, "OK Cliff, make up your mind." And I start the cadence, I go to the left side and I say "Green 20" and I look and I didn't see Cliff. Where the heck did he go? So I go to the other side and I look and I say, "Green 20." But I couldn't find him.

I look down between middle linebacker Lee Roy Jordan's legs and I see another pair of legs behind his . . . it was Cliff. He was hiding behind Lee Roy. I tilted my body to my left, at about the same time he tilted his body to the right, wondering why I hadn't continued the cadence. And our eyes met, and he mouthed the words to me, "I love you."

I snickered and of course now the linemen are yelling, going: "Call the play! Get it going," because they're leaning forward on their fingertips and just about breaking them. I started chuckling. I forgot the play. Luckily, it was a handoff. I kept calling numbers, "Hut one, hut two, hut three" because I couldn't remember the snap count. I eyed Cliff after that, like, "You son of a gun, what are you doing to me?"

I'm not sure if it was the same game, but we came out to pass and it was a pass they had seen dozens of times. I'd fake a handoff to the fullback and throw a quick slant to the split end on the left, Earl Thomas. I did the fake and I came up and Cliff recognized the play. Instead of dropping back into the deep middle, he comes up because he's read the play. So he's broken himself down and he's looking at me. I started into my throw, then I stopped my throw for some reason. I'm not sure how I did it. It felt like I broke my arm. I brought it down and of course then he just went for the ball, where he thought it was going to be.

And then Earl Thomas saw that and just veered to the downfield side of Cliff and went running past him. I just lobbed it over Cliff's head as Earl was running down the field and it was an 80-yard touchdown pass. I don't know why, but I was running downfield. I was just so excited. It's something a quarterback never should do. Cliff was hollering at me all the way down the field, just putting it on me and throwing out all these expletives. "You can't *not* throw that!" Cliff was still hollering at me as we got to the goal line. He just screamed and yelled. And of course I was just laughing, and that fueled the fire even more. Probably eight times out of 10 I throw that ball and he giggles and laughs and says, "I took that play away from you, didn't I?" I'm really surprised he didn't turn around and hit me when we were running down the field.

I looked forward to playing them every year. And then again, I didn't. Because they disguised their defense so well. They'd come up like they were going to blitz, then they'd look like they weren't going to. Then Cliff and Charlie would look at each other, then they'd run back out. I wouldn't tell them I was unnerved, but it bothered me a lot.

You just never knew what they were going to do. I would have loved to sit in on their defensive meetings. Coach Landry must have been awesome to listen to as far as how they prepared for a team. I had great respect for Coach Landry and their whole defense. They didn't do bonehead things—except for Cliff, when I faked him out of his jock.

# Billy Kilmer

## Quarterback

*Teams:* San Francisco 49ers, 1961–66; New Orleans Saints, 1967–70; Washington Redskins, 1971–78
*His View:* Harris's efforts to confuse quarterbacks worked most of the time, but Kilmer figured out one of his fakes.

**C**LIFF WOULD ALWAYS tip a safety blitz. He would always jump around, jump around, and look at me. The time I knew they were going to blitz was when he wouldn't look at me. He would turn his head like he was looking at somebody else, and that was my key and I audibled. Later on I told him what the key was, and he didn't realize he did it.

# Conrad Dobler

## Guard

*Teams:* St. Louis Cardinals, 1972–77; New Orleans Saints, 1978–79; Buffalo Bills, 1980–81
*His View:* Out of his many violent collisions with Harris, Dobler clearly recalls a time when life imitated art.

**C**HARLIE WATERS AND Cliff Harris are good friends of mine now, but when we played it was something else. I remember one time it was almost like the movie *The Longest Yard*.

I ran downfield on a pass play. Cliff Harris missed the tackle. The guy went out of bounds and Cliff was on his knees. I went down there, and I caught him when he was on his knees and hit him, and his head hit first. It was just like the guy in *The Longest Yard.* Remember when he said, "I think I broke his fuckin' neck"? Well, I looked at Tom Banks and said, "I think I broke his fuckin' neck." But I didn't.

The next time I came out, they threw a screen pass and I'm getting ready to square up and Cliff Harris came up and gave me a forearm under my chin and my head hit first. He didn't give a shit about the running back. He knocked the shit out of me.

I got up and said, "Hey listen, how about we just try to finish the game out without killing each other, OK?"

# Paul Warfield

## Hall of Fame Wide Receiver

**Teams:** *Cleveland Browns, 1964–69, 1976–77; Miami Dolphins, 1970–74*
**His View:** *Warfield was always sizing up safeties to find weaknesses, and Harris was among the few who gave him pause.*

**E**VERY TIME I played, I wanted to know if I could get to the post. Could I get over the top and beat the corner and go to the post for the deep ball? There were several safeties around the league where I had to forget about the post because they were so disciplined. They would never be fooled by play action, and they would always recognize what their responsibility was and fulfill it.

The best free safeties were Willie Wood, Hall of Famer . . . Larry Wilson, Hall of Famer . . . Paul Krause, Hall of Famer . . . You just could not get past them. I would include Cliff Harris in that group, too. I would rank him with the top free safeties I played against.

He would not be fooled by some gimmick or play action or whatever. He was always in position. Cliff gave no quarter out there. He was very smart. In addition to that, he would be very aggressive and would play hard and hit hard. As a receiver, you would respect that.

# Craig Morton

## Quarterback

*Teams: Dallas Cowboys, 1965–74; New York Giants, 1974–76; Denver Broncos, 1977–82*
*His View: Morton practiced against Harris and Waters for four and a half years, and then faced them as division rivals with the Giants. So in 1977, when Morton led the Broncos to the Super Bowl against the Cowboys, the safeties had the book on him.*

**T**HEY KNEW ME so well. That was the tough thing. I played against them in 7-on-7 passing drills all the time in Dallas. They knew what I would do and what my traits were. They just knew they could really confuse me.

They knew they could do that because they were protected by the line. So they were able to move a lot and do a lot of things that you'd never see a lot of guys do. They would run up into the line and right up over the center. What kind of audible do you call for that?

We played the Cowboys in the last game of the regular season in '77 when I was in Denver, and I had a hip pointer and I shouldn't have played. There was no reason to play because we had already won the division. But Coach Red Miller said, "You should probably go in and play a little bit." And I said, "Man, Red, if I get hit again it's probably going to explode." And sure enough, Cliff and Charlie came up in the center gap and hit me, and of course my hip exploded again. I was in the hospital the week before the AFC Championship Game against Oakland because of that.

Jack Tatum and George Atkinson of the Raiders, who I played against a lot, they were great. But those two guys, Cliff and Charlie, were also right up there. They called them the Crash Twins or something like that. They would really punish you. You could tell that by looking at receivers going across the middle. They did not want to go in there against those guys. And that helped the Cowboys a lot. Cliff Harris and Charlie Waters were probably the greatest safeties that ever played together.

## Joe Theismann

### Quarterback

*Teams: Washington Redskins, 1974–85*
*His View: One of the more bizarre plays in Redskins-Cowboys history came with Theismann holding the ball at the end of a game at RFK Stadium on a Monday night in 1978.*

**W**E WERE AHEAD 9–3 and there were like four or five seconds left in the game, and our coach George Allen told me to take the snap, run around in the end zone, let the clock expire, then step out of the end zone. Game over, we win 9–5.

Well, everything went according to plan except for one little problem. As I was running around waving the ball in the air and celebrating, I had forgotten to step out of the end zone. Then Charlie Waters and some other guys came in and just knocked the living daylights out of me.

Then a big brouhaha started, with pushing and shoving, lots of "You no-good so-and-so rubbing it in our face" and stuff like that. I was saying: "No, you guys beat me up enough, I don't need to give you incentive to beat me up more." That was one of those classic, you-don't-like-us-we-don't-like-you endings to a football game.

# Jackie Smith

## Hall of Fame Tight End

*Teams: St. Louis Cardinals, 1963–77; Dallas Cowboys, 1978*
*His View: Jackie Smith and Cliff Harris are pals these days, but that wasn't always the case in their meetings twice a year for eight seasons.*

**C**LIFF WAS ALWAYS the commensurate antagonist, but he did it in such a way that you couldn't get mad at him. You could threaten him and you could try to intimidate him, but it didn't do any good—although it made you feel better.

There were numerous times, almost every game, where there was reason to be upset with him. He would just hit you a little late, just to get a rise out of you. He would just hit you whenever he didn't have to. You could retaliate and get thrown out of the game. That was really his ploy, and he did a really good job of it. There were all these little things he would do. There was always something going on, one of us trying to antagonize the other, playing the head game.

Cliff knew that if he could hit me and get me mad it would probably take me off my game a little bit. He and I had a lot of visits on the field and threatened to have a few more off the field after we got dressed and out of the locker room. We finally got over that. I would try to hit him every now and then. If I was blocking and he was coming in for a tackle, I'd try to get him good, too.

He's a great guy and a wonderful competitor. He's one of those guys who really fought you, and so if you can do anything against him you feel good. He was very good at anticipating what was coming.

I got to know him after the game, and what a quality guy he is, and really developed a respectful relationship with him. He's just a great guy. He was a great player and should be in the Hall of Fame.

## Charley Taylor
## Hall of Fame Wide Receiver

*Team: Washington Redskins, 1964–77*
*His View: Taylor remembers some big hits from Harris and Waters, whom he considered the best safety duo he played against.*

**T**HE TOUGHEST HITTER back there's got to be Cliff Harris. He'd get that angle and he'd come in on you. We had some battles. When you look at those guys back there in that secondary, they all could run and they could all hit you. There were days when they would try to shut you down, and you were shut down.

I'll put Charlie Waters in there with Kenny Houston as a safety. They were big guys and they would hurt you. When they smacked you, you felt it. They were strong guys, tough guys, fast guys. You had to give them respect.

As a unit, they were by far the best. There wasn't a lot of talking back then. They were just taking care of their business and knocking you on your butt. That was their thing.

# Harold Jackson
## Wide Receiver

*Teams: Los Angeles Rams, 1968, 1973–77; Philadelphia Eagles, 1969–72; New England Patriots, 1978–81; Minnesota Vikings, 1982; Seattle Seahawks, 1983*
*His View: In one game in 1973, the Cowboys gave up 238 yards and four touchdowns to Jackson—in the first half. Three touchdowns came on long passes between Harris and Waters (who was then playing cornerback).*

**W**HEN I PLAYED against the Cowboys, that was a team I always wanted to beat, because they were always a great team. In that particular game, we had worked on that deep route all week in practice. They were kind of shocked the way it happened, and then the media really blew it up because I said I probably could have scored another two or three touchdowns.

I caught the touchdowns in the first half, so Coach Chuck Knox said, "That's enough for the day." At halftime, the score was 34–14. You say, the ball game is about over at that time. But I'll tell you what, we almost got beat. We were just praying at the time that the ball game would be over. We finally did win it 37–31.

Later on, I still had some good games against the Cowboys, but they were determined to stop me after that. Back when I was playing, anywhere you were on the field they could bop you or hit you or something. They came up and chucked me at the line pretty good. They'd bring somebody out in the flats. They'd double me pretty good the other times I played them.

When Charlie retired from the game, I called him. When I called he knew exactly who I was. Charlie thanked me for getting him off that corner and getting him in there at strong safety.

# Tom Banks

## Center/Guard

*Team:* St. Louis Cardinals, 1971–80
*His View:* Banks was another offensive lineman Harris didn't mind smashing into.

**REMEMBER I CAUGHT** Cliff Harris on a blitz one time and knocked him pretty far out of his pads. And then he caught me one time. I never saw him coming and he caught me right under the chin. I was staggered. I looked around and said, "Was that that little guy?"

He grinned at me after that. We used to laugh about those things. It was a good rivalry. There was never any bad blood or anything like that. He was just tough as can be. He didn't back down from anybody. Cliff would stand in there against anybody. I always had a lot of respect for Cliff.

# Norm Bulaich

## Running Back

*Teams:* Baltimore Colts, 1970–72; Philadelphia Eagles, 1973–74; Miami Dolphins, 1975–79
*His View:* Add Bulaich to the long list of players who felt particularly painful crashes with Harris and Waters.

**THEY DIDN'T HAVE** any fear. They were going to hit you like they want the ball. There was one collision in Philly, I think it was a little swing pass, and Cliff and Charlie, they were coming to kill me. They hit me and I hit them together and they both bounced back.

I went a few more yards and then I was brought down. I hit them pretty hard, but they were coming to knock my head off. Those kinds of people, like Charlie and Cliff and Mel, they were like linebackers in the back.

# CHAPTER 8

# FACING DREW PEARSON

**Wide Receiver (1973–83), No. 88**
**Dallas Cowboys Ring of Honor**

**D**REW PEARSON ARRIVED near the end of Bob Hayes's career, and he quickly established himself as the next big-play receiver for America's Team. Pearson made crucial catches at crucial moments, and he was also a reliable target. He retired as the Cowboys' career leader in catches. (He now ranks third, behind Jason Witten and Michael Irvin.) Pearson was known for precision route running, aggressive blocking, and physical play. The variety of ways he excelled earned him a spot on the NFL's All-Decade team of the 1970s. But mostly, he was known for being the go-to guy when it mattered most. Most famously, he caught Roger Staubach's Hail Mary in the waning seconds of the 1975 playoffs, lifting the Cowboys over Minnesota. Pearson started the lineage of Dallas' great 88s, and he and Staubach became the model receiver-quarterback tandem that would be followed by other 88s, including Irvin and Aikman as well as Dez Bryant and Tony Romo.

# Paul Krause

## Hall of Fame Safety

*Teams:* Washington Redskins, 1964–67; Minnesota Vikings, 1968–79
*His View:* On the Hail Mary, Krause ran from his deep safety position and arrived after Pearson slipped into the end zone. Krause jumped over fallen cornerback Nate Wright, then pointed at Pearson and looked at the officials to register the first in a long series of Minnesota complaints that Pearson pushed Wright.

**D**REW WAS A great receiver, there's no doubt about it, and he did what he had to do to win that football game. Right before that play, there was a fourth-and-16 and Nate Wright got called for pushing Pearson out of bounds, but it wasn't even a push. That was really a big play. That brought it to the Hail Mary pass.

I saw the Hail Mary. I was deep middle. Roger gave a big pump to my right, then came back over to my left. As I'm running over to the play, Drew just pushed Nate in the back. Nate was sprawling on the ground, and Drew catches the ball and that's the end of the story.

I'll say this: Drew made the only play he could make. It wasn't called and they went on to win. Everybody in the stadium, and the Dallas Cowboys, knew he pushed him down, but he did what he had to do and the call went his way.

Nate had him covered. That's all there was to it. In fact, Nate was deeper than he was. To catch the ball, Drew just had to push him over. I've said many, many times that that play was probably instrumental in bringing instant replay into the league. If there was instant replay, we win the game.

We have a big, blown-up picture of the play. Drew got one, I got one, and Nate got one. Drew wrote something like, "It was a great play." Nate wrote something like, "He pushed me." And I wrote something on it like, "Yes, he pushed him." You laugh about it now, but it really hurt. But, you know, all three of us are grown men.

# Jeff Siemon

## Linebacker

*Team:* *Minnesota Vikings, 1972–82*
*His View:* *Siemon was trailing behind Krause, Wright, and Pearson on the Hail Mary play. He remembers watching the play unfold and the Minnesota fans unravel.*

**I THINK THERE WAS** a push. How much of a push, I don't know. Some of those things are called, and sometimes they're not. I'm not shocked that there wasn't a flag thrown. In those situations, many officials are reluctant to throw a flag that will be of that kind of significance. It's easier to do nothing than to do something that will be criticized later. I understand that. It's human.

It was absolutely silent in the stadium. It was just a deafening silence. Someone threw an orange out onto the field, and people were thinking, "There's a flag!" when it bounced through. And then there was nothing. So I think fans were kind of in shock, and then it took a while for it to sink in. And then the boos, and eventually a bottle came out of the stands and hit an official. It was an unfortunate response.

# Tom Pridemore

## Safety

*Team: Atlanta Falcons, 1978–85*
*His View: In 1980 the Falcons made the playoffs for the second time in franchise history. They were home against the Cowboys and led 24–10 in the fourth quarter. Even after Pearson scored to make it a three-point game, Pridemore remembers the Falcons felt confident. Then Dallas put together a drive and had the ball with under a minute left.*

THAT LAST SCORE is a vivid memory for me. We have a blitz called and I'm playing free safety. Billy Joe DuPree was being covered man to man and he breaks free. He runs a slim post right across my face, wide open. I've got to honor that.

The blitz is getting to Danny White, and he throws a major league pop fly. Drew Pearson has a step on Rolland Lawrence and he catches it for the game winner with just 42 seconds to go. It was one of those deals where it went from elation to silence. Everybody's looking around like, "What just happened?" That was a hard one to swallow. That's kind of a sore spot for the Atlanta Falcons organization.

Drew Pearson was one of the guys that you knew in a crunch there was about a 75 percent likelihood that he was going to get the ball. He was their go-to guy. We knew that.

Two years prior to that our season ended in Dallas when Roger Staubach got knocked out and Danny White came in and they beat us in the playoffs. There was a little added incentive. We felt like we were a much better team, and this is a game that we should win. Then it all came crashing down.

The thing that always sticks out in my mind is that we had the ball with about three minutes left. We're up 27–24 and it's third-and-1. If we get a first down, we should be able to run out the clock. We were going to hand the ball to William Andrews.

David Scott, our left guard, takes Randy White about five yards deep into the secondary. Ed "Too Tall" Jones had jumped off sides, but he got back across. But when he got back, he started stumbling across the line of scrimmage. He stumbles all the way down, and when the ball's snapped, he falls into the hole where Randy White was supposed to be and makes the tackle for no gain.

# Ken Houston

## Hall of Fame Safety

*Teams: Houston Oilers, 1967–72; Washington Redskins, 1973–80*
*His View: Houston watched another memorable catch in Pearson's career, a 50-yard game-winning touchdown from backup rookie Clint Longley on Thanksgiving in 1974. Houston remembers Pearson most of all, though, for his tough catches over the middle.*

**T**HAT LONGLEY PASS was a long ball, and when it's away from you, you just watch it take place like everybody else. It just kind of sapped the strength out of us. It was devastating. That was probably the only play that Clint Longley made that I can remember. I think that was his highlight.

Drew made some great catches deep, but most of his catches were when he was the second receiver coming through a zone. I think he took a lot of licks because he would drag across the middle. I give him credit for his toughness. It's interesting at this point that he isn't a Hall of Famer, or at least in that mix. He caught a lot of balls. Drew had the hands. And he had the physical ability to take a hit. So he got a lot of respect.

He was a tough guy. He'd fight you back. He'd get upset and occasionally at least threaten to throw an elbow. At times I think he got tired of knowing we were going to beat on him, and at least swing back or something like that. It made you respect him because, now when you look back on it, it was very, very tough to be a receiver.

If you had a guy with 300 catches back then, it's equivalent to 600 catches now because now you go five yards and you can't touch him. You have to let them catch the ball across the middle and then take a step. What kind of football is that? I don't understand it.

Guys back then, they fought us off the line of scrimmage, they fought us all the way on the route, they fought us all the way across the middle, and they always had somebody like Dick Butkus just hanging in there and waiting there to hit them.

You give him a lot of credit for having the toughness to come across the middle and catch that ball. Once you get back there, it's like seven against one, seven of us against one of him, and we're trying to take our licks on him because we don't want him to come back across there.

# Steve Preece

## Defensive Back

*Teams: New Orleans Saints, 1969; Philadelphia Eagles, 1970–72; Denver Broncos, 1972; Los Angeles Rams, 1973–76; Seattle Seahawks, 1977*
*His View: Pearson's first big clutch catch came the end of his rookie season, against the favored Rams in the 1973 playoffs. The Cowboys were nursing a 17–16 lead in the fourth quarter and facing a third-and-long on their own 17. Preece was covering Pearson and thought he was in perfect position for an interception.*

**T**HE BALL WAS coming and I zeroed in. I thought I had the ball. The next thing I knew I was on the ground and turned around and there's Drew, going for an 83-yard touchdown. It was a good catch. I have a picture from the *Los Angeles Times* of Pearson just basically thinking he's going to get creamed, and instead cornerback Eddie McMillan and I run into each other and just blast each other apart. It changed everything and cost the game. If I pick that off I had a walkaway into the end zone.

Drew was young then. Nobody knew much about him. He just had tremendous moves and the ability to make plays. You could stay with Drew, speed-wise. He was a guy who ran a lot more patterns. He tried to turn you around. He tried to get you out of position. If he wanted to go to the outside, he'd work his way to your outside shoulder so you had no way to get to the ball. He was a master-craft type of receiver. You didn't worry about him running by you. You worried about him making the great catch.

He was a really respectful guy. He would always come over afterward and say, "nice game." It was a different kind of sportsmanship in those days. You respected those kinds of players. Drew was just a remarkable gamer, a guy I wish would have been on my team.

# Roger Wehrli

## Hall of Fame Cornerback

**Team:** *St. Louis Cardinals, 1969–82*
**His View:** *Wehrli and Pearson were both chosen to the mythical All-Decade Team of the 1970s, but Wehrli knew all about facing Pearson for real, squaring off against him for a decade.*

**P**EARSON CERTAINLY WASN'T the burner that Bob Hayes was, but he had good speed. His forte was running patterns. He'd go into the middle and catch it under pressure. He'd have safeties coming in on him and he'd come down with the ball.

He'd always challenge for the ball. Each receiver's a little bit different. As a cover guy, you just sort of watch them all on film and try to figure out their tendencies and work against those.

# Bobby Bryant

## Cornerback

*Team: Minnesota Vikings, 1968–80*
*His View: Bryant's career lasted so long that he knew both Bob Hayes and Pearson well, facing Hayes for seven seasons and Pearson for eight.*

**H**E WAS PROBABLY a little bit meaner than Bob Hayes. You had to watch out for Drew. If the play was away from you and you happened to be loping over in case the play came back toward you, you better watch out because Drew might be headhunting back there.

He was like Paul Warfield, a good downfield blocker, and he'd take a shot at you if he had one. He was a tough player.

Drew was a better receiver than Bob Hayes. Obviously, Bob Hayes was faster than Drew, although Drew could run pretty well, but Drew ran good patterns. He was tough and he would go up and get the ball.

A couple times Staubach ran plays on me where Pearson would come down and run a post pattern, or what appeared to be a post pattern, then he'd break outside. He'd do those double moves, break to the post, and then run outside and Staubach would throw it out there and he'd run under it. And by that time, he'd have three or four steps on us as defensive backs and that's a tough pass to defend. Most of the time our defensive linemen didn't give them enough time to do that, but it did happen.

# CHAPTER 9

# FACING THE DOOMSDAY II DEFENSIVE ENDS

---

**Harvey Martin**
**Right Defensive End (1973–83), No. 79**

**Ed "Too Tall" Jones**
**Left Defensive End (1974–78, 1980–89), No. 72**

WITH ED "TOO Tall" Jones at 6-foot-9 and Harvey Martin at 6-foot-5, the towering bookends of the "Doomsday II" defense terrorized quarterbacks together for a decade. Martin was the more feared pass-rusher. If sacks had been official, he'd have 114 in his career, the most in team history until DeMarcus Ware came along. In 1977, Martin was named NFL Defensive Player of the Year after recording 23 sacks. That would-be NFL record is even more impressive because it came during a 14-game schedule. Martin capped the 1977 season with a pair of sacks in Super Bowl XII, earning him the co-MVP honors.

Jones was Dallas' first-ever number-one overall draft pick. He went on to play 15 seasons, a club record since matched by Bill Bates and Mark Tuinei. He never missed a game. Jones's 224 games played and 203 started are the most ever by a Cowboy, despite taking 1979 off to pursue a career in professional boxing. Jones is Dallas' career leader in fumble recoveries. He's fourth in Dallas history with 106 sacks, unofficially. He'd probably own the batted passes record, if that were an official statistic when he played.

# Jackie Slater

## Hall of Fame Tackle

*Team: Los Angeles/St. Louis Rams, 1976–95*
*His View: As a 20-year Ram, Slater is one of the few people who tops Jones's 15 years with one team. They overlapped enough to go at each other a dozen times, including six playoff games.*

**I**CAN STILL SEE him jumping up, and me standing flat-footed at 6-foot-4½, and the ball being blocked. I was thinking: "How do you defend against this? I'm hitting this guy right in the stomach and he's still jumping up and knocking down the ball."

Ed had this unique ability of reaching out with that long right arm of his and getting his hand on me before I could really get my hand on his body, forcing me to make a commitment with my body. And just as I would do that he would use his athleticism and his fleetness of foot and skip just around me to the outside. Before you know it, he's lying down on my quarterback or putting pressure on him.

He was a very difficult, very awkward guy to block, because he was so tall and rangy. And range is the great neutralizer when you're playing the line of scrimmage. Guys with shorter arms, shorter legs, they probably are going to be a lot more explosive with contact at the point of attack. Guys with longer arms have the ability to absorb the explosiveness of the shorter guys with less range and have more of an impact on them when it comes to moving one another around at the line of scrimmage.

I could never really say I came off and hit this guy and drove him, because he would move one leg back and it covers two feet and all of a sudden the good, solid fit that you had is coming undone and you're chasing or falling on your face trying to keep up as he's moving back.

You were going to get the same guy, the same tenacity, the same smarts, every single time. He was as tactical of a defender, both as a pass-rusher and a run-defender, that I ever played against. So here I was, a big, physical, rangy guy, dealing with a big, physical rangy guy who had a lot of smarts. That's what made him so difficult.

I'll never forget how gracious he was after my first selection to the Pro Bowl, after my eighth year. I remember he came up to me and shook my hand and told me it was well deserved and it should have been some time ago that I made it here. He was just a class guy.

# Terry Hermeling

## Tackle/Guard

*Team: Washington Redskins, 1970–80*
*His View: For eight years, Hermeling battled against Martin. Both were team captains, and both were constantly looking for an advantage.*

I REMEMBER COMING UP to the line of scrimmage on a third-and-8 and he beat me off the ball so bad I thought he was offsides. I started screaming at the ref: "He's offsides! Call him offsides!" Well, he did it a couple more times and I couldn't figure out what the hell was going on.

So I went back and looked at the films. It turned out that just before the snap, Joe Theismann would kick his left foot back. And so Harvey was looking at that left foot, and as soon as that left foot moved, he was going.

So the very next game when we played them, I said, "First pass play, Joe, pull that left foot back but make sure you pull it back early." So Joe does it, and here comes Harvey, offsides. I walked back to the huddle going, "Gotcha," and Harvey just laughed like hell.

We're all looking for an advantage out there. We were very competitive against each other. He was a team captain and I was, too. We'd meet in the middle of the field for the coin toss, and of course he'd be champing at the bit. He was just kind of like a caged animal, kicking at the ground with his feet and kind of giving that scowl look on his face. He was psyching himself up for the game. It was a stare-down; there weren't words, it was just: You better be ready. He didn't have to tell me that, though. I already knew it.

I knew he was going to be coming every play. Harvey was an extremely good pass-rusher, up the field and outside. One of the advantages I had was, that was the only move he had. He did not have a good inside move, so I knew if I could take him away from the outside, I could be successful. Not that I always was, because he was a hell of a player, but he was limited to the outside. If he had an inside move, he would have been phenomenal.

I remember one game he beat me up pretty good. There was like 30 seconds left and we were throwing every down, and Texas Stadium was so loud you couldn't hear anything the quarterback said. So he was beating me off the ball there. But, other than that, it was mostly a pretty good competitive battle between the two of us.

I would never say I dominated him or he dominated me. In football, those are my most cherished memories, playing against the Cowboys. Whenever it was Dallas week, Harvey elevated my level of play. I knew it was going to be intense and it was fun. I'd come out of that locker room two feet off the ground.

# Jerry Sisemore
## Offensive Lineman

*Team: Philadelphia Eagles, 1973–84*

*His View: Losing to the Cowboys was a given for most of Sisemore's career. The Eagles went 6–18 when he was there, including seven seasons when the Cowboys swept the series. Worse yet for Sisemore, he was usually tasked with stopping Jones.*

I T WAS KIND of like the little cartoon where the little kid's swinging at the big guy and the big guy's got his hand on the little guy's forehead, keeping him away. That's kind of the way we were against Dallas.

Coach Dick Vermeil's deal was: What are you doing today to beat Dallas? How are we going to catch these guys? Part of that was my nightmare of number 72 cleaning me up every time. My job was physically impossible. I couldn't even see his numbers, he was so tall. He was 6-foot-9, but he had like a 36-inch waist. He was an amazing specimen. I don't even know how I played against him.

I was blessed with some quickness, so I'd try to just go get him as quick as I could. Even if you could slow him down, you had to figure out how to keep his hands down. It was just kind of a blur. I was 6–4, but it was just physically a challenge. An impossible dream.

He was a rough hombre. He definitely had his game face on every time. He wasn't a guy who would talk smack or anything. I remember after the NFC Championship Game in Philly, he said, "Well, y'all go win the next one." I think that's about all we said to each other.

That NFC Championship Game was our best game against Dallas. Philly has a reputation of having a different attitude. It's beautiful when you're winning, but when you're not, the little kids are disrespectful, the little old ladies are disrespectful, everybody's disrespectful. But on that day, it was amazing. The place was shaking. It was like years and years of frustration was being released. It was beautiful.

# Andy Maurer

## Tackle/Guard

*Teams: Atlanta Falcons, 1970–73; New Orleans Saints, 1974; Minnesota Vikings, 1974–75; San Francisco 49ers, 1976; Denver Broncos, 1977*
*His View: Maurer's final NFL game was a rough one, with the problematic assignment of trying to stop the onslaught from Harvey Martin in the Super Bowl.*

**H**ARVEY WAS THE co-MVP, and I thought I'd get half the car from him because I made him great, but he wouldn't let me have it. He got the car and the ring. He got everything.

Harvey was long and tall and had lots of leverage. He could grab ahold of you and throw you out of the way or hit you with an arm or hold on, and you get the holding penalty even though he's holding you.

Their whole defense messed up our program. That secondary coverage was so good, and when you're facing a guy like Harvey Martin you're not going to hold him out for five to six seconds. It should be two or three, throw that ball, get it out of there. Like when you look at Peyton Manning. He takes two steps and throws. That's what keeps you from getting sacked. It makes linemen good.

The Dallas defense just didn't make mistakes. The gaps were covered and the secondary was making all the rotations they were supposed to, and so that meant a lot of incompletions or sacks or throwing lanes closed. That's all going on while Harvey's hitting me in the head or running his arm under and starting to jump on Craig.

# Tim Irwin

## Tackle

*Teams:* Minnesota Vikings, 1981–93; Tampa Bay Buccaneers, 1994; Miami Dolphins, 1994

*His View:* Jones was so unlike any other defensive end that Irwin didn't know exactly how to approach blocking him.

T WAS LIKE trying to block a very strong spider or an octopus, and you just couldn't do that. He'd put those long arms on you and side-step you. I was a big, strong guy and I wanted to get inside and bang him around, but I couldn't.

If you caught him jumping, you had to try to make him pay, but it was hard to do. Instead of firing off the ball where you could use your bulk and size, you had to take an extra step against him.

I can recall in the 1982 season, it was the first time I ever faced Too Tall. I did not have a good time against him. He was hanging around back there by the quarterback all night. I don't think Coach Bud Grant was too pleased with my performance against him. That first night he gave me fits.

He wasn't the strongest player I ever played, wasn't the fastest player I ever played, but he was one of the best I ever played. I always felt he was very limited by the Dallas scheme. If he were able to use a one-hand stance and go rush around the end, he would have been unstoppable.

# Jim Hart

## Quarterback

*Teams:* St. Louis Cardinals, 1966–83; Washington Redskins, 1984

*His View:* *The Cowboys sacked Hart plenty over his long career, but they didn't get him once in 1975. That was the year the Cardinals allowed only eight sacks. (By comparison, the Dallas record for sacks allowed in a season is 18, set in 1995.)*

THAT WAS ONE of the few years that Harvey Martin didn't wreak havoc with me, because Harvey was a menace on our left side. To think that he didn't sack me at all in those games is really pretty amazing. No question, Harvey was the one I'd see the most of.

Randy would always be getting there late that year. I remember some of them saying expletives as the ball left. They'd knock me down a few times, but they'd always look at me and shake their heads like, "I just can't get to you!"

Harvey, he was just a threat all the time. Much like we tried to do against Lawrence Taylor when he was coming into the league, a lot of times we'd put the tight end on Harvey's side so the tight end would always bump him. We played away from Harvey as much as possible.

The offensive line had such pride. We'd have sackless games and I'd hear them saying: "Let's keep this going. Let's protect Jimmy." At the end of the year I got into it as well because I wanted them to have the accolades, and I would throw it away, probably too soon in a lot of cases. It was eight, but I was only sacked six times. The backup was sacked once, and I think there was a placekick that Jimmy Bakken threw away.

# Vince Ferragamo

## Quarterback

*Teams: Los Angeles Rams, 1977–84; Buffalo Bills, 1985; Green Bay Packers, 1986*

*His View: Ferragamo always had to rush his throws because of the Dallas pass-rushers, particularly Martin. They caused him problems in both of his games at Texas Stadium in 1979.*

**H**ARVEY HAD THE blind side, and Harvey was fast and very elusive. He could speed rush and get through most of the time. So that was always working in the back of your mind. Their speed was the thing. I had just enough time to drop back in the pocket. We didn't run the shotgun. I'd drop back and step up and I'd throw.

You had to make quick reads, and when you hit your back step you wanted to throw it quick. They were all over you. I looked back at some of those games and thought, "Man, there wasn't any time to throw." We held them out the best we could, but they were just so fast, just like Pittsburgh. Those were the two fast teams that really put pressure on the quarterback.

It was kind of funny that my high point and low point against Dallas came in the same season, 1979. In the first game we had a 4–2 record and I was backing up Pat Haden. I came in late in the game because they were beating us pretty good. I finally had a chance to play, but then I broke my hand. They wiped us out in every category, and we ended up losing 30–6.

But then I came back to play them in the playoffs. At the time, I was a young quarterback so Tom Landry would attempt to do some creative things on defense to confuse me. He went to a five-man line. He kind of changed things up late in the game and went to a prevent defense, only rushing three linemen.

I remember one pass that I threw, right before the end of the half, and Randy White hit me when I was throwing the ball deep. I was glad I had a little bit of *oomph* on the ball because he got the best part of me. Ron Smith jumped up between two defenders and caught a touchdown right before the half. That really gave us the confidence going into the second half. The ball I threw to Billy Waddy on that crossing pattern at the end of the game was actually tipped, and we hung on to win it 21–19.

The stars were aligned for us that day. It was early in my career and I just got there, and guys were tired of losing to the Cowboys in the playoffs.

# Eric Hill

## Linebacker

*Teams: Phoenix/Arizona Cardinals, 1989–97; St. Louis Rams, 1998; San Diego Chargers, 1999*
*His View: Hill grew up a Cowboys fan, cheering for the great teams of the 1970s, and he admits to getting a little star-struck once in the league.*

**M**Y ROOKIE YEAR, I was an up back on the field goal extra point team. The first time, I look up, and right across from me is Ed Jones.

After the game—and I've never done this before—but we're walking off the field and I walked up to him and said: "Man, I just want to shake your hand. I know you don't know who I am. But I've been watching you my whole life."

Then I saw him when we were coming out of the locker room and we had a chance to talk. And that was just the greatest. In my eyes, he was just a legend.

# CHAPTER 10

# FACING RANDY WHITE

---

**Defensive Tackle (1975–88), No. 54**

**Pro Football Hall of Fame, Dallas Cowboys Ring of Honor**

RANDY WHITE WAS such a brutal, disruptive force that Charlie Waters dubbed him "The Manster": half-man, half-monster. That monster half stemmed from his intensity, strength, and nonstop motor. Coach Tom Landry actually misused White at first, starting him at linebacker. The Manster truly was born after Landry plugged White into Bob Lilly's old spot at right defensive tackle. Once there full-time, he helped lead Dallas to a Super Bowl victory and earned co-MVP honors. He went on to be named to the NFL's All-Decade team of the 1980s. Along with Harvey Martin and Ed "Too Tall" Jones, White was the core of the "Doomsday II" defense. At 6-foot-4 and 257 pounds, White was quick enough to slip past linemen but strong enough to run them over. If sacks were official before 1982, White would have had 111 in his career, including 16 in 1978. He was durable, too, missing only one game in 14 seasons.

# Craig Morton

## Quarterback

*Teams: Dallas Cowboys, 1965–74; New York Giants, 1974–76; Denver
Broncos, 1977–82*
*His View: Morton wasn't facing just any opponent in Super Bowl XII. The
Cowboys had employed him for nearly a decade, before he lost the starting
job to Roger Staubach and was later traded away. The tough times with
Dallas worsened considerably in the big game, with the Cowboys sacking
him four times (one by White) and forcing four interceptions.*

THE COWBOYS BECAME my nemesis. At crucial points in my
career, they'd come back and haunt me. One real ironic thing was
that the Cowboys traded me to the Giants for a number-one pick, and
that turned out to be Randy White.

The day before the Super Bowl, Coach Red Miller decided he was
going to have a weigh-in for some rah-rah reason. My left guard was
Tom Glassic, and he'd been sick about a week or two prior to the Super
Bowl. He gets on the scale and he weighs something like 230 pounds.
And I was saying, "I'm in real trouble if he's lining up against Randy
White." We had no way to correct that in one day.

Randy White was so quick and so strong. Along with Harvey Martin right next to him, there was no way we could ever stop them. I
was on my back looking up at the tiles of the Superdome ceiling all
evening, and I probably counted most of them. It was a great line, and
then on the other side with Jethro Pugh and Larry Cole and all those
guys. They were amazing.

I've never watched film of that game, but I just remember we had
such a hard time. I probably was hit any time I did anything. They
were just way too quick, especially Randy. I think he just set the tone
for the whole thing. Guys would try to shove him off of Glassic, and

then Harvey comes around the end. I just don't have any adjectives that probably everybody hasn't already mentioned about him.

Those guys were real respectful. They'd smile a lot. When you look up at them and you're on the ground, the great ones smile a lot. Joe Greene did a lot of smiling at me, too. When you talk about the great defensive tackles, you've got Bob Lilly, Joe Greene, and Randy White. It's hard to beat those three guys.

I still see Randy probably a couple times a year, and he's just as jovial as ever. He just loved kicking my ass.

## Otis Armstrong
### Running Back

**Team:** *Denver Broncos, 1973–80*
**His View:** *Armstrong was the leading rusher of Denver's powerhouse running attack that nearly hit 2,000 yards in 1977. The ground game was stopped in the Super Bowl, too.*

**W**HEN I WAS running, there were people where they shouldn't have been—in the backfield. Their penetration was preventing us from running the ball effectively. It's like a blur when you're in a game like that because you don't know who's doing all the damage until you get to the sideline and start discussing it.

Randy and Harvey Martin, we just didn't stop them. They reminded me of another team I played back in those days, the Steel Curtain. They got that kind of penetration with L.C. Greenwood and Joe Greene and all those people.

# Joe Theismann

## Quarterback

*Teams:* Washington Redskins, 1974–85
*His View:* Theismann didn't like the Cowboys one bit, but he loved the rivalry and the fact that playing them was a measuring stick for himself and the Redskins. A big part of those challenges was facing White.

I THINK THE EMBODIMENT of the rivalry—what I call the heart of the lion—was Randy White. Randy set the tempo for everything that happened on the defensive side for the Cowboys. He was nasty. He was dirty. He was physical. He was everything you want in a defensive lineman, and then some. And he was relentless. He'd go sideline to sideline. It was always Randy. If you could control Randy, you could control the Dallas defense.

The respect we gave him was in the 1982 NFC Championship Game. At the end of that game, I stepped into the huddle and called the play, "Spread right, 60 Outside." Russ Grimm, my left guard, said, "No." I said, "What do you mean, no?"

He said, "I want to run 50 Gut right at Randy." I said, "Coach wants 60 Outside." He said, "I know, but I want to run 50 Gut." Now I'm middle management, OK. I've got to make a decision. I've got my coach calling one play and my teammates calling another. So I ran 50 Gut. We gained five or six yards. I look to the sideline, Coach Joe Gibbs signals in 60 Outside. I step in the huddle, put my head in the huddle, call 60 Outside and Russ goes: "No. I want to run 50 Gut." We run the play again, get the first down. I think we ran six consecutive plays right at Randy. Right at him. Because if we could control Randy, we felt like we could control the line of scrimmage. Now, they had John Dutton, Ed "Too Tall" Jones, Harvey Martin—they were a serious front four. But Randy was the catalyst of it. I think that's the way we looked at it as a football team.

He and Russ Grimm were in some of the greatest battles. It's only fitting that both of them are Hall of Famers. These were two warriors going toe to toe, at a time when you could be very physical in the game of football.

Today it has changed completely, for offensive linemen and for defensive linemen. We actually practiced hitting, which is contrary to the philosophy today. We actually practiced contact, to prepare ourselves for contact and battle. Today it's "You push, I push, I'll run by you, maybe you won't."

I don't remember the exact game, but I do remember Randy giving Mark May a rabbit punch in the back of the head after we scored a touchdown. Randy just gave him a forearm right in the back of the head. And that kind of thing just punctuated the dislike that we had.

They pummeled me one year down in Dallas. I have a picture that was in *Sports Illustrated* where I got hit by three of them. The good thing was they hit me simultaneously so it was like one big whack, as opposed to separate ones. That was a picture that I actually got framed, just to remind myself of how much I didn't like them.

They knocked me out of a game down in Dallas, I think they broke a collarbone and a couple of ribs. I got hit high by Ed, and I think low by Randy, and wound up lying on the field, gasping for air, looking up at that stupid hole in the ceiling.

# Steve Kenney

## Guard

*Teams:* *Philadelphia Eagles, 1980–85; Detroit Lions, 1986*
*His View:* *By 1981, the Eagles were tired of double-teaming White, only to watch him build a personal highlight reel by crushing quarterback Ron Jaworski over and over again. Philadelphia's solution was moving Kenney, their best pass-protecting guard, to the left side. Still, White remained their number-one worry.*

**W**E WOULD GET the game plan for Cowboys week and they would label the positions. They would put a T for tackle and an E for end. Then they'd put an M for Randy White, for the Manster. They didn't call him a tackle or an end, just M. They didn't change the letters on anybody else. We didn't really laugh about it, either, because it was serious business. The M was scary.

The first thing Coach Vermeil talked about was Randy White. He'd draw the big M on the blackboard for the Manster and he would keep talking to me: "What are you going to do, Steve?" It was a week that was treated totally differently than the rest of the season. They were like playoff games to us.

Randy was strong, but mostly it was the speed and intensity. He was the most intense player I ever played against. He just had kind of a nonstop kinetic energy. I remember hearing Coach Vermeil say "Randy White starts a war on every play."

His feet moved so fast. It reminded me of needles on a sewing machine, just chop-chop-chop. He could embarrass you every play. I heard a story of him before I got there where a guy got hurt and the backup came in and Randy got three sacks in the quarter. He could just wreck the whole game.

If Randy didn't make the tackle during the play, he'd smack you after. It was like the play lasted a few seconds after the whistle blew.

We used to sit around and wonder what kind of drugs he was on out there because no human could be that intense. But he wasn't taking anything. It was just his natural DNA.

I remember one play when he was rushing the passer and Jaworski threw a little pass across the middle to a receiver named Scott Fitzkee. White turns around from rushing the passer, and 30 yards downfield leapt on Fitzkee's back like some kind of tiger in the wild. He ran a wideout down and leapt through the air and just mauled him to the ground. Most defensive linemen wouldn't even think about going after the wideout. They'd just turn around and watch. But he took off. People don't do that. I've never seen anybody do that.

On pass plays, everybody had a swim move, but nobody else had it at his speed. He was the quickest guy I ever played against. Just when you'd start waiting on that, he had this move where he'd do a double-fist-punch up under your chin that could knock you over on your back. He had his knuckles taped up real thick. I can remember after playing him the bottom of my chin being sore.

It was either the first or second time I played him when he beat me so bad on one play. He started out way on my outside shoulder, and when I slid out to pick him up, he took one step straight upfield. Next thing I knew, this bolt of lightning went right by me. He beat me clean, and it was a sprint back to Jaworski. Coach would usually let you have it when you gave up a sack, but that time he just said, "Well, that's just a great move by a great player." He moved so fast on that play that they probably figured nobody could block him.

I missed a defensive back on a safety blitz one time because I was so focused on White that I didn't even notice the guy walk up. He wasn't three feet from me. That was a play where we had an interception because that safety got in there and hit the quarterback.

Randy would complain about holding a lot. He would fuss and kick and scream like crazy: "He's holding me! He's holding me! He's holding me!" We were playing in Philly one time and I got a holding call and my buddy Stan Walters was yelling at the ref: "Why are you calling a hold on him?" I looked at Stan and said, "Stan, I tackled him." And he said "Oh, never mind."

When we would have interceptions, as offensive linemen, we were supposed to run over there and make a tackle. When we played Dallas, I had to look at the defensive back who made the interception with one eye, and I had to keep the other out for Randy White. He would loop around the field and use that interception as an excuse to try to take me out of the game. It was like he was a heat-seeking missile and he was going to get rid of me. One time he did that in Philly, and you can see it on film. He ran about 20 yards just to get the right angle on me. They blew the whistle and he was still about five yards away, and I guess he figured if he'd run that far he wasn't going to do it for nothing, and he still hit me. We got in a little shoving match. He did it usually where he wasn't going to get a penalty, but it would be at an angle where I didn't see it coming.

I played against him more than I'd like. I hope he at least has one bruise on his body somewhere from me. I think so much of Randy White now, although I didn't really back then. I'd like to see him today and shake his hand and congratulate him.

To me, we weren't playing the Cowboys. I was playing Randy White. It was that big of a deal. He was the best defensive tackle I played against, and nobody's in second place. I think for a time there in the late 1970s and early 1980s, he was hands-down the best defensive player in the NFL. He was probably the best player in the NFL. You just don't call a defensive tackle the best player, but I think he was.

# Tom Mack

## Hall of Fame Guard

*Team:* *Los Angeles Rams, 1966–78*

*His View: You'd think nine years of facing Bob Lilly would prepare you for White. For Mack, that wasn't the case.*

**T**HEY WERE CERTAINLY two of the best I've ever played. Randy changed the game for me because I had to worry about him just trying to run over me. Bob would try to run around you. Randy was strong enough, and he was fairly short and stocky, so it was more like playing a wrestler. I didn't do as well blocking Randy because my forte was quickness and agility like Bob.

Most of the time Randy would try to bull rush me and I had problems. He was just a master at using his strength. I'd go for his legs as much as I could. If you can work on a guy's legs, then they get a little bit apprehensive. You can keep people off-balance with that. To me that was much more how you had to play Randy.

He was very aggressive, but he was not a dirty player or any kind of a cheap-shot guy. He'd come hard, but that's what everybody was paid to do, was go hard.

# Randall Cunningham

## Quarterback

**Teams:** *Philadelphia Eagles, 1985–95; Minnesota Vikings, 1997–99; Dallas Cowboys, 2000; Baltimore Ravens, 2001*

**His View:** *Cunningham spent a lot of time trying to avoid White early in his career. He didn't fare so well in a 1986 game, as White had one and a half of Dallas' 10 sacks on Cunningham that day.*

**H**E WAS ALWAYS wreaking havoc in the backfield. I used to hate that part about him. I always had to be aware of where he was.

There were a lot of memories of him coming up that middle and me getting out of the way. There was no sitting comfortably back in the pocket when I went up against him.

I think that his motor was the thing that kept him going. You could tell he was committed to the job at hand. He was under a great coach. He was a blessing to the Cowboys. He was all about business. He would just get things done. He was a guy I wanted to go up to and shake hands with after the game.

# Blair Bush

## Center

*Teams: Cincinnati Bengals, 1978–82; Seattle Seahawks, 1983–88; Green Bay Packers, 1989–91; Los Angeles Rams, 1992–94*
*His View: In 1983, the Seahawks had grown from an expansion team to a playoff team. Late in the season, the Cowboys showed them their line still had some work to do before the postseason. Dallas sacked Dave Krieg eight times, including three and a half by White. Bush spent much of the day trying to slide over and help undersized guard Reggie McKenzie slow White.*

REGGIE WAS TOWARD the end of his career and playing at about 245 pounds, and Randy White was a lot bigger, stronger, and faster. Most of the time we were trying to get some help over to that side. We were trying to double, but Randy was so powerful and quick that sometimes I couldn't even get over there quick enough.

He was very intense, in great condition, and stronger than most people. He was a load for anybody when you get that sort of size and strength differential at the height of his career. I remember Randy was one of the first ones who got a lot bigger than everybody else. He was in the weight room more and played with more intensity.

Right about that time a lot of guys were focusing more on weight-lifting. They just were a lot bigger and stronger. You can neutralize a guy like that, but every once in a while you're going to get caught in an off-balance situation. I think almost every offensive lineman has one of those nightmare games that tend to stick in the memory more than the ones where you had a really good one. I don't think you can talk to an offensive lineman who hasn't had at least one.

# CHAPTER 11

# FACING TONY DORSETT

**Running Back (1977–87), No. 33**
**Pro Football Hall of Fame, Dallas Cowboys Ring of Honor**

TONY DORSETT WAS one of the greatest running backs in NFL history, and if it weren't for Emmitt Smith he'd be the best Dallas back ever. He trailed only Walter Payton on the career rushing yards list when he retired. He currently ranks eighth, just ahead of Jim Brown. Dorsett held most every Dallas rushing record until Smith came along, and now he ranks second in several categories, including rushing yards, attempts, touchdowns, and 100-yard games. Dorsett was a constant threat to break the big play. He took off for five of the Cowboys' nine longest runs from scrimmage: 99, 84, 77 (twice), and 75 yards. Dallas sent a first-round pick and three second-round picks to Seattle to draft Dorsett, and it paid off instantly. He won Rookie of the Year honors and led Dallas to a Super Bowl title over Denver. Dorsett ran for more than 1,000 yards in eight of his first nine seasons. The only time he didn't was the strike-shortened 1982 season.

# Herm Edwards

## Cornerback

*Teams: Philadelphia Eagles, 1977–85; Atlanta Falcons, 1986; Los Angeles Rams, 1986*

*His View: Edwards came into the league with Dorsett and ran after him his entire career in Philadelphia, including his 206-yard game as a rookie. (If you watch Dorsett's highlights, you can usually see Edwards's No. 46 running after him.)*

**W**HEN YOU MEET guys in those college all-star games, you're kind of linked for the rest of your life, because of all the time you spend with them. It was great being around Dorsett. He really had a great personality. A lot of guys called him Flip Wilson because he kind of looked like Flip Wilson. He was special, and you respected him.

You always had a fear of his ability to break the big run. He broke a couple big runs on us, I can remember. He had an 84-yard run against us as a rookie. Man, it was a long one. If Tony got to the back end of your defense, look out. He was fast. He ran for the tough yards, too. He wasn't afraid to run inside.

One thing about Tony Dorsett—he hit the hole. He didn't mess around. One step and he was running downhill. You see the play against Minnesota, the 99-yard run, but he was more than that one play. He'd run for three, he'd run for four, he'd run for five.

It was the explosive run that was the backbreaker. Those big ones always started in the middle of the field. You see all the great runners, it starts with the hash mark, then they run to the numbers, then they get outside the numbers and they're on the sideline and you can't catch them. A lot of his runs were that way. If he got his shoulders squared up and got to the back of that secondary, you better look out because it was going to be a big run.

If I tried to compare him to a more modern player, I'd say Jamaal Charles. I drafted Jamaal Charles, and Tony was kind of like that guy. I would compare them a little bit. Tony was a little stockier than Jamaal. Jamaal was a little better at catching the ball. Tony could catch it, but they didn't ask him to do it a lot.

I always liked playing against Tony and Dallas. You had to go through Dallas if you wanted to go to the championship game. And we finally got past them in 1980. We beat them in the NFC Championship Game. Roger Staubach had left then, but they still had Tony, they still had a pretty good team, and they were still the Dallas Cowboys.

Back then, for some reason, they struggled when they had to wear the blue jerseys. So we wore white at home to make them wear blue. We were ready to beat the Cowboys. There was so much electricity in the stadium. We finally beat the Dallas Cowboys—and not only that, but we beat them to get to the Super Bowl. To me, that was bigger than the Super Bowl.

## John Swain

### Defensive Back

*Teams:* *Minnesota Vikings, 1981–84; Pittsburgh Steelers, 1985–86; Miami Dolphins, 1985, 1987*

*His View:* *Swain was one of several Minnesota defenders with a shot at Dorsett on his record-setting 99-yard run on January 1, 1983. On the video of the play, Swain is No. 29, and you can see him try to grab Dorsett at about the Dallas 15-yard line.*

**I**T WAS JUST like any other play. You just don't expect them to go 99 yards. But we were able to come back and put some drives together and all of a sudden win the game. Here's what I keep telling folks: I don't remember the 99-yard play, but I remember winning. That play just doesn't go away, though, because they keep showing it on highlights.

You always have to be going to the ball against Tony. If he gets out there, you're not going to catch him. So you always have to be coming to the ball, you've got to slow him up, and always pay attention.

Tony Dorsett, personally, I've always felt that he was one of the top backs in the league. I used to tell people about how the speed he had was just unbelievable. It was just crazy speed.

## Joe Greene

### Hall of Fame Defensive Tackle

*Team: Pittsburgh Steelers, 1969–81*
*His View: After Dorsett's first three runs went for nine, 16, and 13 yards, it was clear to Greene and the Steelers that they were facing a new dimension in their second Super Bowl against Dallas.*

**T**HAT WAS ONE series that I recall quite vividly. The Cowboys got the ball first and they were moving the ball really, really well. Dorsett was creasing us, and he was doing bad things to us. They moved the ball to about our 35-yard line. And then they did a gadget, a gimmick play, and they fumbled it and we recovered it.

It was a long ball game, but I think that was a big, big, pivotal point in the game. It was very likely that they would have gotten a touchdown or a field goal. I always felt the team that scored first in the Super Bowl had a significant edge because of the magnitude of the game.

Them scoring first could have impacted the outcome. Obviously I'm speculating, but that was a big play.

We had a difficult time corralling him because he was so quick and so fast. He was not only quick and fast, he was quick to get fast. He was a darter and a cutter and had amazing strength, but you never did get a real good hit on him. No matter where he was on the football field, he scared you because he had the ability to hit a crease and hit his head on the goal post, as they say.

I remember a trap play, I think it was the left guard and he trapped me and I missed Tony, and the play went probably for 15 or 20 yards. He was just a tough guy to get your hands on because of his speed and quickness. No doubt the window was slim to get him when you were on the line.

We fancied ourselves on being very simple on defense. And I think that helped us a lot against the Cowboys, because they would do a lot of motions and trying to create mismatches. And with all the shifting they did, we didn't try to run with them, we didn't try to move with them. We always said regardless of how much they move, they had to stand still a couple seconds before they snapped the ball. Then we would make our adjustments from there, not try to make them on the move.

I was thinking about it and I can't ever remember making a tackle on Tony. I sure can't. Usually Tony was beyond the line of scrimmage when he got tackled. That was probably an area where I couldn't get to him.

# Jack Ham

## Hall of Fame Linebacker

*Team: Pittsburgh Steelers, 1971–82*

*His View:* Dorsett's presence in the second Dallas-Pittsburgh Super Bowl meant a different kind of preparation and discipline for the Steelers.

**W**HEN YOU HAVE a guy in the backfield who could go the distance any time, it made you really concentrate on staying in your lanes. You couldn't run around blocks because you're going to give Dorsett an opportunity to cut back and make plays that another running back would not make.

I don't think people realized how tough of a runner he was, too. He would run inside. It wasn't just the great speed he had. We were very conscious about being disciplined and not letting him get that 45- or 50-yard run like he was able to do against a lot of people.

Dallas didn't have a game-breaker like that in the backfield the first time we played, somebody who could explode into a hole and turn a play into something big, a great cutback runner.

We felt we had to stop him first before anything else. Trust me, everybody on our defense was pretty conscious of where he was. There weren't that many running backs who could do what he could do. He was that special.

# Charles Mann

## Defensive End

*Teams: Washington Redskins, 1983–93; San Francisco 49ers, 1994*
*His View: Mann very nearly made Dorsett's highlight reel, and one of his teammates started his own Hall of Fame highlight reel after somehow catching Dorsett.*

**I**F WE WERE blitzing and bringing the linebackers, that meant the ends would take the running back if he goes out for a pass. One time Mel Kaufman was blitzing on my side, and therefore when Dorsett flanked out I had to cover him.

We practiced this all the time. It was no big deal in practice when you're running with Brian Mitchell or somebody mimicking Dorsett. Well, it happened in a live game, and here comes Tony Dorsett.

I was hanging with him initially. He wasn't running that fast, since he's the third or fourth option. And then he looks to see who's covering him, and then he turned on the jets and took off. He was like: "I got a defensive end following me? I'm out of here."

He got by me by about five yards at least, and I'm freaking out and running as hard as I possibly can and they throw the ball and it was overthrown. So I covered Tony Dorsett! I came back to the huddle and was huffing and puffing because I had to run about 40 yards. I said, "Oh gosh, I hope they don't go back to that." It was scary.

When he was running, he was as good as they come. He just squirted out on runs a lot. We needed to make sure we kept him in check so he didn't burn us with big plays. For the most part he didn't, but he was so good. I was a childhood fan of his, and it was a thrill just being on the same field as him and playing against him, and seeing how smooth he was. Yet he was so efficient as a running back.

I played in the game on September 5, 1983, where he took off out of the backfield and Darrell Green came from across the field and got him after a 77-yard run. Nobody knew who Darrell was yet. He was starting as a rookie, and we knew and respected him, but then the world got to see it on that play. He walked Tony Dorsett down, and Tony Dorsett was not slow. It made Darrell's career.

# Ted Hendricks

## Hall of Fame Linebacker

*Teams: Baltimore Colts, 1969–73; Green Bay Packers, 1974; Oakland/Los Angeles Raiders, 1975–83*
*His View: Hendricks didn't see Dorsett often during his 15-year career, but he recalled being frustrated by him in a loss to Dallas in 1980—the same year the Raiders went on to beat the Eagles in the Super Bowl. Dorsett had 121 total yards and a touchdown in Dallas' matchup against Oakland.*

THERE WAS A gliding that Dorsett had when he hit the hole, and he had the smoothness and an innate ability to look and find out what the blocking scheme was doing and choose his way out. He didn't break anything on us, but he sure did gain a lot of yards.

He won the game for them. We couldn't stop him. He was running up the middle against us all day. I think it was a great credit to the offensive line. He was breaking a lot of tackles and finding the holes.

It was like five yards, 10 yards every carry, it seemed. I didn't have that much of an opportunity to tackle him because I was on the outside. Maybe I was on his back sometimes when he was going up the middle.

# Jeff Siemon

## Linebacker

*Team: Minnesota Vikings, 1972–82*
*His View: Siemon faced Walter Payton twice a year, so he was used to ganging up to take down a runner. It was something the Vikings failed to do on Dorsett's 99-yard run during Siemon's final regular-season game.*

**I**N THE OLD days we'd call him a scatback, a guy who had tremendous speed and quickness. Walter Payton might be a counterpart. Both were fast, but Walter was a load. He weighed 210 pounds but he ran like he weighed 250.

Tony Dorsett went down a lot easier than Walter Payton, but getting to him was a task. He was probably as elusive as any back in his day. He had a great offense that he worked with and an excellent offensive line, and those guys need to take some credit for his success.

With a guy like that, you always had to gang tackle. There's just an added emphasis on not quitting and making sure there were four or five people around the ball. He was a great cutback runner, too, so we tried to be cognizant of our position as the ball's snapped and players are flowing to the ball. If there was a little hole he'd find it, then all of a sudden he was in the secondary, then he could break it almost any time.

On that 99-yard run, it was like letting the air out of a balloon in the Metrodome. That was my last season, and we played some 3–4 defense, so I can't remember if I was on the field or if Scott Studwell had come in. I think I was on the field for that, but I don't remember. Maybe I forced myself to forget.

# Johnnie Gray

## Safety

*Team:* Green Bay Packers, 1975–83
*His View:* Gray often grew frustrated with Dorsett, because it was always hard to hit him just right.

**W**HEN YOU CAME up to hit him, you had to make sure you were moving your feet, that you kept your low center of gravity.

He wasn't one of those guys who you just throw your body and he's going to go down, because he had that low center of gravity.

More than likely you were just going to get his shoulder pads, because he always ran low. He always ran under control and he always had that burst of speed. You had to be careful, or you'd make the highlights.

Once he got through, it was a touchdown. If you watched throughout his career, there wasn't really anybody who had a true shot on him. If guys didn't hit him right, and didn't wrap up, then more than likely he was just going to fall off and Dorsett would get extra yardage. Now they call it yards after contact. Back then it was just hard-nose running.

*Extra Point*

# America's (Most Hated) Team

The Dallas Cowboys became so popular that it also became popular to root against them. Perhaps the leader of the Down with Dallas movement was coach George Allen, who plied his venom on both coasts just as Dallas was becoming a perennial contender.

"George Allen decided he was going to make Dallas public enemy number one," said Tom Mack, a Hall of Fame guard for the Allen-coached Los Angeles Rams. "He really created that rivalry and tried to throw it into the face of players to try to get them riled up."

After hating the Cowboys in Los Angeles from 1966 to 1970, Allen landed in Washington in 1971, where ownership and fans already despised Dallas and were quite receptive to ratcheting up their hostility.

Defensive lineman Diron Talbert often led the charge. He famously taunted, needled, and criticized Roger Staubach after the Redskins' win over Dallas in the 1972 NFC Championship, and for many years beyond that game.

"Diron was head of the Let's Get Roger Pissed So He Doesn't Think About Throwing the Football Committee," former Redskins quarterback Joe Theismann said. "George Allen would direct Diron Talbert to get under Roger's skin any way he could—call him names, do anything you had to do. I think the only time Roger ever lost his temper was against the Redskins."

Allen's successors in Washington continued the Cowboy-hating, Theismann said, and that added to the joy of defeating Dallas in the 1982 NFC title game.

"Beating the Dallas Cowboys, at home, in RFK Stadium, was the biggest thrill I ever had in football," Theismann said. "Now, winning the Super Bowl was sensational. But to beat the Cowboys at our place, in front of our fans, with our fans pounding on these aluminum seats and the ground shaking beneath your feet, that was something to behold. It wasn't just playing for the NFC Championship, but you were doing it playing the Dallas Cowboys, the hated Dallas Cowboys, our archrivals."

The differences in style also fed the Cowboys-Redskins rivalry. In Theismann's era, the Cowboys were known as the glamorous finesse team, while the Redskins pounded out victories on the ground behind a group of linemen called the Hogs.

"We never considered them tough," Theismann said. "They were great athletes, but they had these shiny little pants. You know, they just irritated you. It's like the kid that pulled up with the sweater that was tied around his neck when you were in high school. We truly did not like them. They didn't like us. I didn't play golf with Roger Staubach in the off-season. There was absolutely no love lost."

Charles Mann broke into the league with Washington as a defensive end the year after the Redskins beat Dallas in that title game. It didn't take him long to jump into the rivalry.

"Everybody wanted to knock them off their pedestal, but nobody wanted to knock them off the pedestal more than the Redskins," he said.

Late in the 1983 season, the Redskins and Cowboys were both 12–2. Mann was among several Washington players who made a military-style "march" into Texas.

"We all assembled in the back of the plane just like in *Stripes* with Bill Murray, and we marched off the plane," Mann said with a laugh. "TV cameras were there and it made the Dallas news that night, further inciting the rivalry."

Of course, the hatred is mutual among Cowboys fans. And they love to remind the Redskins of their superiority.

Like on September 9, 1985, when the Cowboys crushed the Redskins 44–14 and Theismann threw five interceptions—on his

36th birthday. When he left the game in the fourth quarter, Dallas fans gave him one more present.

"I sat on the bench, and the entire stadium started singing 'Happy Birthday' to me," he said. "It was one of those times where you wished it was a grass field instead of artificial turf so you could crawl under a blade of grass."

And there was the time in 1979, after the Cowboys edged the Redskins 35–34 for Staubach's final victory, when Harvey Martin delivered a funeral wreath to the losers. (The wreath had been sent to Dallas from the Washington area before the game.)

"Harvey threw it into our locker room, and that was just one more thing that sort of punctuated the rivalry," Theismann said.

"Had I been within distance of him when he threw that in there, we would have been in a fight," said Terry Hermeling, who typically lined up against Martin. "You don't go into another team's locker room and pull that kind of crap. I really thought that was out of character for him."

The Philadelphia rivalry has had its moments as well, especially when Buddy Ryan coached the Eagles.

In 1989, Dallas coach Jimmy Johnson insisted Ryan put a bounty on Troy Aikman and Luis Zendejas, a kicker who left the game with a concussion after linebacker Jessie Small blasted him after a kickoff. Two years earlier, the Eagles led 30–20 very late in the game and Ryan called for Randall Cunningham to fake like he was taking a knee then throw a long pass.

"It was Buddy Ball," Cunningham said. "When we were playing Dallas, you could say it was revenge, but I'd say it was, 'We're going to get one up on you.' Whether it was embarrassing you or whatever it takes, that was the coach he was. As players, whatever he told us to do, we carried it out.

"The thing with Dallas was, there was a hatred. We did not like the flashy star on the helmet. We did not like their fans filling up one-third of our stadium and rooting loud."

Not all the rivalries were in NFC East, though. The Steelers, 49ers, Packers, and Vikings also have had their moments with Dallas.

In the early 1990s, the 49ers-Cowboys rivalry heated up as the teams clashed in three straight NFC title games—the winner of each going on to win the Super Bowl.

"You hated them because there were times they stole your glory, and vice versa, when we stole theirs," former 49ers tight end Brent Jones said. "It's weird, everybody thought this game was like the Super Bowl, and they were right."

After the 49ers rivalry began to fade in the mid-1990s, Green Bay became the little brother trying to knock off the Cowboys in the NFC. They failed a few times before finally ascending while the Cowboys slipped away. While those Packers teams went on to become champions, they never had the pleasure of taking out the Cowboys along the way.

"Coming from the Packers side, it sucked because you don't want to hear, 'We're America's Team and blah, blah, blah,'" former Packers nose tackle Gilbert Brown said. "You just hate to lose to a team like that. But you know, I'd rather lose to a team that has great players, great coaches, great respect for the game, rather than some bum team."

# Section 3
# The Triplets

**B**Y THE LATE 1980s, America's Team was on empty. Super Bowls and winning seasons seemed like ancient history. Even the great Tom Landry no longer had the answers, his team sinking to 3–13 in 1988. Then oilman Jerry Jones bought the Cowboys and decided to remake America's Team. He started out by replacing the quiet, straight-laced Landry with one of Jones's old college teammates at Arkansas: Jimmy Johnson, the loud, vein-poppingly intense coach from the University of Miami.

Jones and Johnson went backward at first, with the Cowboys going 1–15 in 1989. Yet like the debacle of the franchise's inaugural 1960 season, this actually was the start of something great. Michael Irvin had been the last first-round pick of the Landry era, and Troy Aikman was the first pick of the Jones-Johnson era. In the middle of the 1989 season, the Cowboys pulled off a blockbuster trade that sent Herschel Walker to Minnesota for several players and draft picks—including the pick used to take Emmitt Smith in 1990.

The Cowboys returned to the playoffs by Johnson's third season and were back in the Super Bowl the next year. They won back-to-back Super Bowls in dominating victories over the Buffalo Bills in 1992 and 1993. Growing tensions between Jones and Johnson boiled over after that second title, prompting Jones to bring former University of Oklahoma coach Barry Switzer out of retirement to coach the Cowboys. The Triplets won one more Super Bowl under Switzer, defeating the Pittsburgh Steelers after the 1995 season.

## FACING AMERICA'S TEAM

While the Triplets were the shining stars of the revitalized Cowboys, they were supported by a massive offensive line that featured Larry Allen, Erik Williams, and Nate Newton, as well as a strong defense highlighted by Charles Haley and Deion Sanders.

# CHAPTER 12

# FACING MICHAEL IRVIN

---

**Wide Receiver (1988–99), No. 88**

**Pro Football Hall of Fame, Dallas Cowboys Ring of Honor**

**M**ICHAEL IRVIN WAS essentially impossible to cover, and he gladly let everyone know it. He used his 6-foot-2 frame to overpower defensive backs. He had one of the most accurate quarterbacks in NFL history. And he played in a perfectly balanced offense that nearly always guaranteed single coverage. The result was dominance that led to three Super Bowl titles and a rewriting of the team's receiving records. With his fiery personality, Irvin put the swagger into Dallas' rebuilt powerhouse. He was widely considered the heart and soul of the 1990s Cowboys—on and off the field, for better or for worse—and he was chosen to the NFL's All-Decade team of the 1990s. While he was the Cowboys' emotional fuel, he also piled up impressive numbers. Over a five-year stretch, he averaged 90 catches, over 1,400 yards, and eight touchdowns. His 65 receiving touchdowns are second only to Bob Hayes in team history.

# Eric Davis

## Cornerback

*Teams: San Francisco 49ers, 1990–95; Carolina Panthers, 1996–2000; Denver Broncos, 2001; Detroit Lions, 2002*

*His View: For a three-year stretch in the early 1990s, the Super Bowl was essentially played a couple weeks early. From 1992–94, Dallas and San Francisco met in the NFC title game, with the eventual AFC opponent offering meager resistance. Dallas won the first two clashes and Davis faced Irvin all three times.*

EVERYBODY ASSUMED THAT Mike did a lot of talking. He may have to other guys, but not to me. We'd walk out there and he'd holler out on that first play, in that rough, rough voice he has, stick his hand out and say, "E.D., let's go to work." And we'd slap hands, and then we'd play.

In those first couple of plays, he'd kind of push me from behind, he'd try to grab my arm, or slap me in the head. He'd head-butt me. That was his thing—he loved head-butting. And then I'd have to hit him in the throat, and that was it. It was like, "If you want to fight, we can fight; if you want to play, we can play." He'd try me every single time. I love those games, to this day. It was competition at the absolute highest level.

I played in an era where we had great receivers and great cornerbacks and great quarterbacks. And Troy Aikman was the most accurate guy out of the bunch, in my opinion. I can't tell you how many times I was covering Mike on a slant route and I was all over him. And his fingers would be extended three inches farther than mine and Troy would put the ball in that three-inch window. And he would do it every single time. If I didn't knock the ball down, Mike, on the receiving end, was not going to drop it. So I had this guy throwing darts to a guy who had super glue on his hands.

For a defensive back, it doesn't get better than that. Not only that, the games we played mattered. Our rivalry began because you had two storied franchises. And rivalries don't start until I beat you or you beat me when it matters.

In 1992, when they beat us, I think to a man, we thought we were a better team. We felt like we let one slip away. In the '93 game, that wasn't the case. I truly feel that if we would have played those guys another 12 quarters, it only would've gotten uglier. That was the best team I ever played against in my life. That offense was a machine. It was like taking body blows. It was like standing with your back in the corner, up against the ropes, and Mike Tyson in his heyday, just punching against your ribs. And we'd go to the sideline and yell and scream at each other and regroup: "We know what they're doing. Let's execute. Let's fix this."

And then we'd go back out on the field and here we'd go again. We're standing with our feet on the 2-yard line. And they're handing the ball to Emmitt, and here's big Nate Newton running around the corner. Or Erik Williams was coming at you. And it didn't stop. It was like an avalanche. You could hear the rumble, you could hear the trees cracking, and you could see it coming, and there was just no escape. This was just the best team I had ever gone against. They flat-out beat us.

That feeling did not leave. That taste was ever-present, from the moment the time went off the clock in that title game in 1993 until we had an opportunity to see those guys again. We knew we were going to see them again, and we had to see them again.

In 1994, when we get out there on the field, the stadium was crazy. The crowd was wild. I'm looking at the guys and the atmosphere was exactly what it was supposed to be. You had the two best teams; it was like the Super Bowl. I personally think you had two of the best teams ever.

That '93 Dallas team was the best team I ever saw in my life. My '94 team was assembled to beat that team. It took a team of All-Stars. You could never assemble that team again. You can't afford to assemble that team we had in '94. I would put that team against anybody. You had Hall of Famers everywhere, and we were averaging 40-something points in the playoffs.

On the interception early in that 1994 game, I took off running straight to what they had shown me on film in that situation. Troy threw it. I caught it. I scored. And that right there changed the game. It let them know we were prepared to play that day. It let my guys know we were prepared to play that day. The entire sideline, everybody knew that, OK, this is a different game. In '94, we were better. That was the best team we ever played against in '93, and the best team that I know anything about is our '94 team. That's how good those guys were. That's what it took to beat that team.

You hear all the time about physical receivers, but the term "physical receiver" is an oxymoron. If guys like contact, they play defense. Receivers don't want to get hit. But Michael Irvin was truly a physical receiver. He wanted to bang, he wanted the contact, he wanted to get his body on you.

Michael tells me now that Norv Turner would tell him, "You got to play big on this play." Because he would run that skinny post and he would run it between the corner and the safety, and he would take a lick. And they would tell him, "Mike, I'm sorry, but you're going to have to take the lick, but you got to make this play." And he had the heart to go and do it. A lot of receivers, they don't do that.

If the game was played then the way it's played today, where you can't hit guys in the middle of the field like we used to, Michael would have had 2,000 yards a season, easily. Because those seam routes we used to kill him on, they couldn't hit him today. He would be a defenseless receiver.

He's the best player I ever played against at getting off the jam at the line of scrimmage. Jerry Rice was the best route runner. Cris Carter: best hands. Mike wasn't the fastest guy; he wasn't the quickest guy. He would just always do his job every single play. He ran a 4.5 the first play of the game. The issue was, on play number 75 or 80, the last play of the game, he was still running a 4.5.

He was efficient, he played hard, he played smart, and he was a flat-out winner. That's why they called him the Playmaker. I wish he would have been my teammate.

## Aeneas Williams
## Hall of Fame Cornerback

*Teams: Phoenix/Arizona Cardinals, 1991–2000; St. Louis Rams, 2001–04*
*His View: Williams faced Irvin twice a year for nearly a decade, and he recalls the precise moment when he knew the battles between the two eventual Hall of Famers were going to be intense.*

**D**URING MY ROOKIE year, he caught a 17-yard in route on me, and I caught him from behind and punched the ball out and recovered it. The next series Michael came off the line and gave me one of the hardest forearms you could ever deliver across my head. Just not being moved by that blow across the head, and getting right back in front of him and competing, it started a very good clash. Even though I was 5–10, I was very physical and willing to compete. And he was going to try to intimidate.

He was a very good route runner. He had very good body control. He also knew how to shield you off of fade routes. He had very good hands and an awareness schematically of what you were trying to do to him. And he knew that, most times, because of the successful running game with Emmitt, we would be in one-on-one situations.

One of his favorite routes was to go about 17 yards and then go on what we call that skinny post, and Troy Aikman would hit him in stride. Michael wasn't afraid to go across the middle. He wasn't afraid to go after deep balls. Michael was a complete receiver.

Dallas was very simple. You knew there was a handful of plays you were going to get. When you went on the field with them, they were probably going to do some of the very same plays, with Moose Johnston coming through and leading Emmitt, and Erik Williams and Larry Allen and all the big guys coming downhill. Even though we didn't win a lot of games, we always played the Cowboys strong.

In my fourth year, when Buddy Ryan was here and Rob Ryan was my defensive backs coach, Rob encouraged Buddy to put me on the opposing team's best receiver. That's when I was assigned to Michael the entire time. Chan Gailey would try to move him around and create matchup problems. Once I started being assigned to him it didn't matter. One time he was put in the backfield, and then they'd motion him, but I had to follow him the entire time. Or we'd create defenses where it was almost like in basketball you'd call a box-and-one.

In 1998, when we finally made the playoffs, the Cowboys had beaten us in both regular-season games. And they were predicted to beat us again. I just remember it vividly because I was shadowing Michael the whole game. If he went to the restroom, I was assigned to him. You had to work first by competing with Michael all over the field, and then after that by making a play on the ball. I was able to intercept Troy Aikman twice, and we went on to upset them. It was the most memorable experience that I ever had in football. I was in press coverage against Michael. On one of the interceptions, Michael tried to run a corner route and Troy tried to get it over the top of me and I was able to jump up, catch it, and get two feet in bounds. On the other one, they tried to run a curl route, and Troy tried to throw the ball at a low point where he thought I couldn't get to it. But I was able to drive on it and get my hands underneath it in order for it to be a completion on the interception.

When I was covering him, it was bump and run, and he would try to push off. Michael would do anything he could—within the rules, and maybe even a little against the rules—and do anything he can to get the edge.

In his mind it was always: You're not going to stop me. You're not going to press me at the line of scrimmage, and if you do, I'm going to do something—slap you across the head or something to try to intimidate you to get you off of me—so I can get to where Troy's throwing the ball.

Who won? I think it's like a fight when the referee lifts up both hands. All I know is, Michael helped bring out the best in me. He helped bring out the competitive fire, as well as the willingness to prepare.

# Jerry Rice

## Hall of Fame Receiver

*Teams: San Francisco 49ers, 1985–2000; Oakland Raiders, 2001–04; Seattle Seahawks, 2004*

*His View: The Cowboys-49ers rivalry was big, and Rice considered his rivalry with Irvin big, too. They were competing every week, whether their teams were playing each other or not.*

**H**E USED TO look at the newspaper to see what I did that Sunday, and I'd look at the newspaper to see what he did. And if Michael had one of those big days, man, it pissed me off. I wanted to outdo Michael Irvin and he wanted to outdo me.

When you're playing against him, you can't help but to sit on that sideline and watch a guy that you knew was going to make plays and make a lot of noise. I really enjoyed watching him play, the way he could run his routes and position his body and almost block out defensive backs to make those catches.

143

# Eric Allen

## Cornerback

*Teams: Philadelphia Eagles, 1988–94; New Orleans Saints, 1995–97; Oakland Raiders, 1998–2001*

*His View: Allen came into the league the same year as Irvin and they faced each other twice a year for seven straight seasons. The challenge was physical and mental, and the buildup began well before kickoff.*

IT STARTED THAT Monday or that Tuesday, when we started to break Dallas down, and it happened on both teams. Their guys would give it to Michael, "Hey, you're facing EA this week—he's going to shut you down." And my guys would do the same thing, "Oh, you're facing Michael, he's going to kill you this week." They knew about the friendly rivalry that me and Mike had, and they really wanted to make sure their guy won it, so they got you pumped up that week. Whoever was playing Michael in practice would take on his whole personality. He'd come to the line of scrimmage and talk and say: "Come up here and press me! Don't be afraid! Don't back off!"

Of course, you know the Eagles fans were always crazy, and they wanted you to do well. So if you were in the grocery store or wherever during the week, they'd tell you: "Hey, get on Michael! Get on 88 this week!"

The big thing with me facing him was just the physical nature of the game. You knew you were going to battle. You were always going to be in the spotlight, and it was going to be competitive. It was going to come down to a couple plays between me and him that would swing the momentum either one way or another. If he caught a ball on you, you would hear it. He would tell you, "All day." It was a friendly back-and-forth. I would tell him: "Hey, is this the best you got? I practiced all week for this; is this the best you got?"

There was the timing and rhythm of his routes, and he had the long, graceful strides. And just like most Hall of Fame guys, he had a great intelligence. He knew the game, and he understood what was going on, why things happened, the X's-and-O's part. He could line up and have a great understanding of what defense we were in, what I was trying to do to counteract what he was doing. So, although it was a physical battle and that's what he's known for, it was also a mental battle.

Him and Troy had such great rhythm that they could basically run routes and not really look at each other. We began to understand that and jump that. So instead of running the out route, he would run kind of like a semi-post; we called it a glance route, because he would run, and on his fifth step he would look in and the ball would be there. It was almost unstoppable. You can't take that inside position, because you're giving him the whole rest of the football field. They were forcing the corner to play outside of Mike. Troy understood that. So he would throw this glance route, and because Mike was so big, he would jump up and shield the ball. There's no way a cornerback—I don't care how big you were—could knock the ball down. If you weren't careful, he'd run through your arm tackle. So after seeing this in a couple of games, I'm like, "Wow, that is an unbelievable route." I mean, that's unstoppable. They could throw that every time.

But then I adjusted. What I did was, when he was at the top of the route, at the top of the numbers, I would line up outside. But on his third step I would jump inside, and I would break it up. They would look at me like: "What the heck is going on? There's no way." Because Troy would basically throw this ball blind. He would drop back and on his fifth step let the ball go. So then they started adjusting on the route against me. Years later I talked with him, and he said, "Oh, we knew you knew that route and we started adjusting a little bit." Those are a few of the things that are a little outside the game that make every little thing worthwhile, if you understand that the battle isn't just physical. It's a mental battle, it's a preparation battle, and if I can force them to adjust, and if they can force me to adjust, that's just another sign of respect about our game. There was this constant evolution of what you're doing during the process of the game.

You appreciate a guy who enjoys playing the game. And Mike, you know, he never cheated the preparation, he never cheated the giving 100 percent on the field. I have so much love for him and being a true competitor and football player.

It was so frustrating playing a guy with his kind of talent, because he could jump up, he could run by you, he could run through you, he was a great blocker, he had a great understanding of the game. It's like you talk about tools with the guys in baseball; he had all the tools you needed to be a Hall of Fame receiver.

# Troy Vincent

## Defensive Back

*Teams: Miami Dolphins, 1992–95; Philadelphia Eagles, 1996–2003; Buffalo Bills, 2004–06; Washington Redskins, 2006*
*His View: After Eric Allen left the Eagles, Vincent took over the role of Philadelphia's Irvin stopper. Only, this rivalry wasn't as friendly as Allen-Irvin.*

**M**IKE HAD A nickname in our locker room. We called him The Boogeyman. The Boogeyman, like kids are all scared of him, like, "The Boogeyman's going to get you." How do you get the reputation of The Boogeyman? You put the film on and watch people play against him. He was scaring us to death.

"The Boogeyman's coming to town this week!" That's what our defensive coordinator Emmitt Thomas used to say in the back of the room with the defensive backs. If you just watched the tape, oh, people were afraid. They wanted no part of that.

You watch the tape and he's smacking people in the head, he's grabbing people, he's intimidating people. You can see other defensive backs being intimidated and not challenging him. So you said to yourself, "If I want to be the best, I got to perform against this guy." You knew you were going to be in a brass-knuckles fight against a guy who is going to impose his will on you for 60 minutes.

He presented such a nightmare matchup for 90 percent of the guys he played against because he was three, four, five inches taller, 20–30 pounds heavier. And he was mean. I was big, like Mike, and I could run. So, this was kind of an Ali-Frazier kind of fight. I'm 6–1 and 200 pounds, and if he punches me, I'm going to punch him back. If he grabs me, I'm going to grab him back. Let the official call it. It was a fight. We fought all the time.

Before the game, the officials knew what it was going to be. I knew what it was going to be. Mike knew what it was going to be. We're going to bang. Either I'm going to win or you're going to win or they're going to throw us out of this game. I can be honest with you today: He didn't like me, and I didn't like him. We didn't even shake hands after a contest.

I was a different person during Dallas week: not talking, very little food. His physical presence, there was nobody like him. During that time, you had Michael, you had Cris Carter, you had Jerry Rice, and they all gave you something a little different. Michael, he wanted that contact.

And if you didn't give him the contact, it was pitch and catch because No. 8 was throwing BB's. So if you didn't come up and try to squeeze Mike, it was like Troy was playing 7-on-7. If you didn't go up and cut that and reduce that air and put a hand on him, it was pitch-and-catch for Troy.

Pushing off, that was just part of the game. If you didn't get that close to him, you didn't have a chance because Troy was so good, they were so good together. That was the only way you had a chance, but then he's going to hit you with that body. Mike was a real tough grinder. He was the number-one physical receiver. Most receivers try to out-finesse you. Most didn't want that contact, and Mike invited that.

Him and I, we didn't say one word to each other on the field. Not one word. He used to have what I called a big, ol' pacifier in his mouth. It never came out, but I would try to make every attempt to get it out of his mouth.

Who would ever imagine me and Mike today? We're doing church together and talking about how we're raising our boys together. We're sharing information. He's my brother. Nobody in their wildest dreams would ever think they would see the two of us sitting together in church, praying together, hugging each other, at dinner together. No Eagles fan would ever think that was even humanly possible.

# Mark Collins

## Cornerback

*Teams: New York Giants, 1986–93; Kansas City Chiefs, 1994–96; Green Bay Packers, 1997; Seattle Seahawks, 1998*
*His View: Collins felt obligated to teach Irvin what he should and should not do when he arrived in the NFL, then battled him twice a year for five more years.*

**I** REMEMBER WATCHING HIS film when he came out of Miami and also in the pros, and he'd get down in a three-point stance and look at the quarterback. I saw him do it a couple games in the NFL and I thought, "Why isn't anybody hitting this guy?" I thought, "If I see him do it I'm going to can him." Sure enough, he got in a three-point stance, and I canned him. I got him good. He was on his back. He was like, "Oh, good job." It was like, "Welcome to the league, rookie," and that was it. Then he comes out the next play and starts to do it again and then he stands up because I taught him a lesson: This ain't college.

Michael Irvin was a hell of a receiver. I have total respect for a guy like that—always willing to compete, always worked hard. No matter what happened off the field, you were getting 100 percent from that kid every single down. I tried to mix him and Troy up. So if I could get those guys off the same level, I think I did my job.

Michael had a couple touchdowns on me, no doubt about that. But my job was to eliminate the total big play. I didn't want the snowball effect. You know, one touchdown leads to two touchdowns leads to three touchdowns and next thing you know you're on SportsCenter and everybody's talking about how bad you are.

## Willie Williams

### Cornerback

**Teams:** *Pittsburgh Steelers, 1993–96, 2004–05; Seattle Seahawks, 1997–2003*

**His View:** *How's this for pressure on a cornerback: Williams was in his first year as a starter, in his first Super Bowl, and facing Irvin during his best season.*

IT WAS EXCITING, and it was going to be a great challenge. I used to watch Michael Irvin as a fan before I got into the NFL. I just liked the way he played the game. He gave 100 percent, and I liked the showboating, the way he performed after he scored a

touchdown. But when he played against me he never scored a touchdown—you don't want anybody scoring on you and next thing you
know they're dancing.

Michael Irvin's so strong, and he wouldn't let you get your hands on
him. But we practiced so much disguising our coverage and we would
surprise him coming down on him and get physical. We had to take
it to him early to let him know we were going to be physical all game.
We had to throw off their timing routes because their offense was all
about timing. If he had a free release, Troy Aikman had an opportunity
to throw the ball every time.

If the ball wasn't coming his way, he said a little something, but not
toward us. He'd be telling Troy: "Throw me the ball! He can't cover
me!" Stuff like that. But he was really vocal motivating his guys. I could
see him in the huddle, talking to his guys, getting them ready to play.
He was definitely being like that cheerleader out there. He kept that
going throughout the game. And of course the guys all bought into it.

We fought hard, we had an opportunity, but we just fell short. They
knew what to expect during the Super Bowl and during that week.
They were probably a little more prepared for that Super Bowl than
we were.

# Jason Sehorn

## Cornerback

*Teams: New York Giants, 1994–2002; St. Louis Rams, 2003*
*His View: Irvin talked a little trash to some opponents but not to others.
Sehorn was in the group that would hear a thing or two from Irvin.*

**T**HERE WAS A little talk but not too much. You know receivers love to talk. He'd come out there and jaw-jack you. But they were kicking butt, so it made it a little easier for them to speak their mind. I would butcher the eloquence of his trash talk if I tried to repeat it, but it was basically reminding you all the time of:

**A:** How inferior he thought you were because you couldn't stop him and that this is going to happen all day long. Or . . .

**B:** He'd tell you what he was going to do next. He could come up and say, "I'm going to run a skinny post right here." And you couldn't stop it. Because if you guessed it was a skinny post and it was a fade route, touchdown. If he ran the skinny post, you still couldn't stop it because the timing of the throw and catch with him and Troy was perfect.

He wasn't a burner, or somebody you were afraid was going to just run by you. But, somehow, he was always open. Granted, he played with a Hall of Fame quarterback, but, still. He was just a real competitor. Some guys didn't like it when it wasn't thrown their way, but Michael *hated* it when it wasn't actually in his hands.

I would say that by measurables, the way we look at some of these receivers now, the more athletic ones—Randy Moss, Calvin Johnson—they're so athletically gifted. They're big, they're fast. But Irvin, I'm not taking anything away from him, but if you tested him in the vertical and the 40 and stuff like that, I don't think he'd be like a Calvin Johnson. But, production-wise, oh my gosh, it's like, his competitive nature is what separated him from everybody else, I thought.

# CHAPTER 13
# FACING TROY AIKMAN

Quarterback (1989–2000), No. 8
Pro Football Hall of Fame, Dallas Cowboys Ring of Honor

**TROY AIKMAN WAS** the general at the controls of the most powerful offense in the league, calmly, methodically, and masterfully directing a series of precision attacks. Between his understanding of the offense, his poise, and his pinpoint accuracy, defenders knew they had very little margin for error—and that even when they were in the right defense there was a good chance Aikman would beat them. Aikman earned the respect of teammates and opponents for his toughness and his willingness to be part of a winning formula, leading an offense that featured the guy who would become the leading rusher in NFL history. As the leader of a balanced football team, he didn't rack up yards like Tony Romo and he didn't lead comebacks like Roger Staubach. Aikman's teams regularly jumped out to big leads and pounded teams into submission with late-game handoffs to Emmitt Smith. However, on those instances when big passing days were needed, Aikman was certainly capable. He threw for over 300 yards 17 times, four of those in the playoffs.

# Eric Allen

## Cornerback

**Teams:** *Philadelphia Eagles, 1988–94; New Orleans Saints, 1995–97; Oakland Raiders, 1998–2001*

**His View:** *Aikman lost his first six games to the Eagles and took some hard beatings along the way, and then Allen watched him grow from punching bag to dominant rival.*

TROY WAS ONE of the best leaders at the position that I ever played against. He had a great rhythm, a great confidence, and a great poise about him. And his toughness was off the charts. Those are the things you really can't measure.

If he played for any other team outside the Cowboys, I'd be excited for a guy like that, to go through all those trials and tribulations and sorry teams of 1989 and 1990 to finally win three Super Bowls.

He was the one guy who held that team together. He had Michael, Emmitt, Jay Novacek, that great offensive line, Alvin Harper. All those guys were great. But the buck stopped with Troy. That's why they were so successful. That's why they were able to win multiple championships. They had a leader who wasn't afraid to get dirty, wasn't afraid to get in anyone's face; no matter how emotional Michael was, or Emmitt, Troy would keep them in check.

His throwing motion and the quick release were a lot like Dan Marino's, but he was a sturdier, stronger guy. His foundation was a little bit better than Marino's. He was a big, physical guy. When that ball came out of his hand, you knew it was going to be an accurate throw. He wasn't going to put his receiver in a situation where he could get knocked out. So we had a lot of respect for his accuracy.

That's the one thing you can't really hurry. When a quarterback is accurate, all he needs is time. And after Troy got time, that's when he became that potent guy. There was no spot on the football field he couldn't get the ball to. If there was one thing he was as good at as anyone, it was being accurate under duress, not being afraid to stand in the pocket when the pocket's collapsing and there are 300-pound guys coming at him. He would step right up and make an accurate throw.

Those were the kind of things that separated him from everyone else in my playing days. He was a little like Tom Brady is right now; he had that kind of leadership and aura about him. When he came onto the field it was like: "Man, this is a star. This is the real deal. This is Troy Aikman, and he's the quarterback of the Dallas Cowboys."

Troy didn't have any ups and downs emotionally like everyone else. If something went wrong, he'd never let it linger. Like Brett Favre, I could pick him off and look back at him like: "Why'd you throw that? You know I'm going to pick it off if you give me something." But Troy, he was dialed in. He was always on to the next play, good or bad. As much as you kind of look back, and want to see him slam his helmet or look at the linemen, he would never do anything like that. He was always just focused, straight ahead, next play.

I never saw him rattled. Frustrated, yeah—jumping on guys because they didn't do the right thing, yeah—but rattled, no. There were just a handful of guys you couldn't rattle. There are a lot of guys you could send multiple blitzes at and then, after being pounded four or five times, it's lights out, game over. No, you couldn't rattle Troy.

In the game in 1991 where we sacked him 11 times, they wanted to pull him out. We were pounding the guy, and not once did he flinch or give any kind of sign that he was defeated. He would get up and go back to the huddle and we were like, "Man, this guy's tough."

# Clyde Simmons

## Defensive End

*Teams:* *Philadelphia Eagles, 1986–93; Arizona Cardinals, 1994–95; Jacksonville Jaguars, 1996–97; Cincinnati Bengals, 1998; Chicago Bears, 1999–2000*

*His View:* *Simmons recorded four and a half of the Eagles' 11 sacks in that 24–0 Dallas loss in 1991. The year before, he ended Aikman's season early on a big hit.*

EVERY TIME HE got hit in the 11-sack game, his reaction was like, "You know what, I've got to get up and do my job." That's what made it like an another-day-at-the-office situation. He didn't get up complaining, he didn't get up and slam the ball or anything. He just got up and kept playing.

You could see the frustration on his face like, "I can't get anything done." But he didn't say anything. You could just see from his body language that he was frustrated about not being able to lead his team to a win.

I've got nothing but a lot of respect for Troy. After I knocked him out for the season in 1990 and he had to have shoulder surgery, the press in Dallas were trying to crucify me and say I was a dirty player. But Troy came out and said: "I just happened to land on my shoulder. There's nothing dirty about the play." He took the high road. Football has injuries, and he took it as, "It just happened to be me today."

# Mark Collins

## Cornerback

*Teams: New York Giants, 1986–93; Kansas City Chiefs, 1994–96; Green Bay Packers, 1997; Seattle Seahawks, 1998*
*His View: Collins was always fascinated by how seamlessly Aikman directed the balanced and disciplined offense.*

TROY FIT THE Ernie Zampese-Norv Turner offense. He was their perfect guy. Everything's off a basic read, off a five- to seven-step drop. I would say he was really good at pre-reading defenses, but he was great at reading defenses while dropping back.

And that's why you'll see, once he sets that foot, pretty much the ball's gone. He was great at that. So that's why I always moved a lot. With Troy Aikman, Dan Marino, even John Elway, you always had to move because those quarterbacks could really read.

I always moved a lot on the corner. Our secondary, we'd do a cover two shell or come up and jam the receiver or other things; we always mixed it up. Troy, he would look at me very often, and that's when he'd try to get his read. Once he gets his read off the safeties, he wants to know if I'm in zone or man or two-man trail. So if I could just give him that little bit of doubt and make him throw the ball somewhere else, I did my job. But, Troy was really good at that, so Troy would find Novacek or a back out of the backfield or Alvin Harper or something like that. You know, football is not a chess match. It's a game of checkers, because the moves come quick.

Of course, he was a tough quarterback, too. He proved that even going back to UCLA. I saw some games where he got hit right on the chin and came back and got right up and played. In the NFL, this kid, he took a beating his first year. He got his ass kicked, but he kept getting up. We thought, "Man, he's tough. He's going to be something once they put the pieces around him."

I never saw him throw a wobbly pass. Never. It was always a perfect spiral. Boom. Boom. Like a gun. Boom. Boom. And it's always in a spot where the defensive back can't get it. I don't know what his quarterback rating was, but I'd say he was about 98 percent right on where to get the ball to.

One time he threw the ball to me—and I dropped it. I anticipated that skinny post that they do, but I dropped it, and I thought, "That's going to come back and bite us," and it did. I had the pick right there, and I dropped it. It's like missing a layup.

# Troy Vincent

## Defensive Back

**Teams:** *Miami Dolphins, 1992–95; Philadelphia Eagles, 1996–2003; Buffalo Bills, 2004–06; Washington Redskins, 2006*
**His View:** *It was hard enough for Vincent to fight with Michael Irvin on every play, but also reading Aikman—while Aikman was expertly reading him at the same time—could make his job even more frustrating.*

**T**ROY VERY SELDOM puts the ball in a place where he gives a defensive back a chance to actually pick the ball. When you look at a lot of Michael's catches, it was always just in a place where he was going to catch it or it was going to be an incomplete pass. He always knew what you were going to do to him defensively, so you weren't going to trick him on schemes. He threw a nice ball, a really nice pass. He had a lot of arm strength. He had the whole package.

Your primary goal against Dallas was to manage that run. You got to control the line of scrimmage. To do that, most people put an extra man in the box to just manage the run. You got Daryl Johnston and Emmitt Smith back there. And so a lot of times you're in one-on-one coverage. That's when quarterbacks are just looking and thinking: "Where's the one-on-one coverage? That's where I'm going." If your technique wasn't right, there wasn't much of a chance to make the play or get an interception. The numbers were against you. And if you tried that and didn't succeed, you were probably looking at the back judge throwing up the hands for a touchdown or a first down.

There's a perception when you watch the tape that, "Man, I can get to that ball." On tape it's not like he's zipping that thing out there. Then when you get in the game and it's real life, it's coming out much quicker than it's looking on tape. In reality it was like, OK, this ball really is coming out and it's coming out fast. They had this down to a science.

As a defensive back, you have to take calculated risk. You're thinking: "OK, the pass-rush is going to be there. If the pass-rush gets there I got about two seconds, two and a half to three seconds, and then that ball is going to be where he's going." The receiver is still running his route, but the ball's already left his hand. So you have to honor what you're seeing in front of you, and then the ball's gone. And it all happens in an instant. It's either a completion or a touchdown. You're going: "I'm going to get this one . . . I'm going to get this one." And then you go for it, and you're a fingertip or an inch or two away from getting there. It can be frustrating.

I think I got him once or a couple times. But there wasn't one time where I could say, "I really got him."

# Corey Miller

## Linebacker

**Teams:** *New York Giants, 1991–97; Minnesota Vikings, 1999*
**His View:** *Miller chased after Aikman twice a year for seven seasons, but he often couldn't catch him.*

**I GOT A PICTURE** hanging on my wall right now. A guy made a painting, actually, of me getting ready to hit Troy Aikman and sack him. A lot of people ask me, "Well, did you sack him?" I say, "No . . . but I did hit him." I hit him right in the chin. I hit him good. I should have knocked him out. But, he'd be bloody and he'd stay in there. He's one of the toughest quarterbacks I've played against. You couple that with the smarts and all the talent around him and his ability to get rid of the football and he's one of the best ever.

You think about the amount of talent and personalities that he was surrounded with. I think that team was poised because of Troy Aikman. Even when you had them in trouble, had them on the ropes, they were struggling a little bit, he was always the calm one.

When Michael was going crazy with the antics, Troy would get in Michael Irvin's face and say certain things to calm him down. There was such a great admiration and respect from his teammates. That's what it takes when you're a leader. Regardless of personality, they calmed down and listened to Troy Aikman.

# Willie Williams

## Cornerback

**Teams:** *Pittsburgh Steelers, 1993–96, 2004–05; Seattle Seahawks, 1997–2003*

*His View: Covering Michael Irvin in a Super Bowl, as Williams did, was plenty difficult. It was even more challenging because Aikman seemed to know everything that was happening on the field.*

**T**ROY AIKMAN MADE you be careful with your eyes. He would look you off and throw in another direction. He had been playing the game a long time when we got to that Super Bowl, and you just had to be careful.

You couldn't always see how he'd do it on film, because he'd lull you to sleep. He knew every route everyone was running. He knew where everyone on the field was going to be. He didn't throw it to the receiver. He threw it in the area where he could go get it. He was just a great, smart quarterback who was hard to prepare for.

He was a student of the game, as most quarterbacks are. And the good ones watch a lot of film. They know all about the corners the receivers were going up against, how they align, their weaknesses, their strengths. I'm pretty sure he knew that not just for us, but for all the teams he played. You could tell during the game because he would barely make a mistake.

The thing about Troy Aikman is, you've got to get pressure on him. You can't let him sit back there and give him too much time, because he'll definitely pick you apart.

# Mark Kelso

## Safety

*Team: Buffalo Bills, 1986–93*
*His View: Aikman ruined Buffalo's third try at a Super Bowl win with an MVP performance, most memorably with a championship-sealing*

*outburst—two touchdown passes to Michael Irvin within an 18-second span that put the Cowboys up by 18 points at halftime.*

**T**HOSE TWO TOUCHDOWNS were crushing to your spirit, because we felt like we had a great opportunity in this game.

The thing I recall most about Aikman was that the offense was really efficient. He had a really strong arm, and his accuracy was pinpoint. It was an offense that had everything you needed, and a quarterback who had poise and threw it with velocity. He was a guy with great poise and didn't get flustered. He thrived under the pressure and was able to maintain that even keel. He had a lot of confidence, and I think that spilled over to his teammates.

He seemed like a real unselfish player. I'm a big proponent of having a balanced offensive operation, and they had a great one. It takes a special quarterback sometimes to fit into that role. Sometimes they want to throw the ball around 40 times a game, and he seems like he was more focused on making sure he led his team to victory as opposed to putting up the biggest numbers.

## Ernie Mills

### Wide Receiver

**Teams:** *Pittsburgh Steelers, 1991–96; Carolina Panthers, 1997; Dallas Cowboys, 1998–99*

**His View:** *Mills watched Aikman finish off his Steelers in the Super Bowl, then got a taste for what it was like to catch passes from him in Dallas.*

**I** WOULD BE RUNNING the same kind of routes I had been running for seven years. But as soon as you turn your head it was like, wow, it's right there. You couldn't help but think, "What would happen if I had this guy all my career?"

# Jerry Gray

## Defensive Back

*Teams: Los Angeles Rams, 1985–91; Houston Oilers, 1992; Tampa Bay Buccaneers, 1993*
*His View: Gray faced Aikman twice in Aikman's first two seasons. As a rookie Aikman threw four touchdown passes, and the next year he went over 300 yards with a pair of scores to Michael Irvin.*

**W**E KNEW WE were going against a young guy and that the Cowboys weren't as good numbers-wise. But they competed against a really good team—and we had a really good defense then. Even though they lost that game when he was a rookie and they were 1–15, they competed. And that's where you measure players.

You could tell that he was going to be a guy who was poised in the pocket, who understood how to read coverages. That's good for a young quarterback. You were talking about a big, strong guy, a young pocket quarterback who can throw the ball down the field.

I played left corner on first and second down; then I played safety on third down. I just know that he was reading a lot of good stuff. He was doing some things you didn't think a lot of rookies could do. When you got to the end of the game and went back and looked at it, you could see this guy was going to be good.

# Jason Sehorn

## Cornerback

*Teams: New York Giants, 1994–2002; St. Louis Rams, 2003*
*His View: Like a lot of cornerbacks, Sehorn felt helpless to stop Aikman at times, regardless of how well he was covering Irvin.*

**T**HAT'S A DEMORALIZING feeling as a corner when you've got really, really good coverage and you're thinking, "I can make a break on this ball" and it should be knocked down at worst and picked off at best, and then you end up making a tackle. It frustrates you, but it also motivates you. You have to think, "OK, I have to go find a way to stop this."

It didn't matter how well you had the receiver covered. That ball was thrown low and away. So you could break on the out route perfectly, and all of a sudden the ball keeps sailing away and away.

He just was a doctor with the ball. Some of these quarterbacks now just have cannons and they can wing it and their receivers go make great plays, but he put the ball where you couldn't get to it.

# Charles Mann

## Defensive End

*Teams: Washington Redskins, 1983–93; San Francisco 49ers, 1994*
*His View: Mann knew how important it was to somehow get Aikman or Irvin out of sync.*

**W**E KNEW THEM well. We knew they would run the ball down our throat. We knew that if Darrell Green couldn't hold up on

Michael Irvin, we were going to have a long day. We knew if we could disrupt Irvin just a little bit that that would also disrupt Aikman.

Aikman really never had to win the game with his arm. He just needed to manage the ball well, and he did. If you didn't get to him and he got the ball off, it was probably caught. That's very frustrating. So your goal was to hit Aikman, knock him around, throw off his timing.

# Jessie Tuggle
## Linebacker

*Team: Atlanta Falcons, 1987–2000*
*His View: The key to the great Dallas teams was all pretty simple, if you ask Tuggle.*

**T**ROY WAS SO cool. He sort of reminds me of the way Brady plays. He had the arm strength, he studied the game, he was a total professional, and he went out there and played every game like it meant something to him.

The team was loaded. But if you don't have a quarterback that's ready to go like Troy Aikman, you don't win a Super Bowl. What else can you say?

# CHAPTER 14

# FACING EMMITT SMITH

---

**Running Back (1990–2002), No. 22**
**Pro Football Hall of Fame, Dallas Cowboys Ring of Honor**

EMMITT SMITH WAS the most productive running back in NFL history, setting records for rushing yards and rushing touchdowns. His Hall of Fame resume includes three Super Bowl victories, a Super Bowl MVP, a league MVP, and numerous other records. All of that from a guy many thought was too small to be an every-down back in the NFL. Once Smith arrived and completed The Triplets, his impact was immediate. He won the NFL Rookie of the Year award, and the Cowboys very nearly made the leap from a one-win team to a playoff team his first year. Smith was selected to the All-Decade Team for the 1990s. He shares a spot on that mythical roster with Barry Sanders—which is fitting because they are often compared. Their very different running styles make it the perfect sports-bar discussion. Hypotheticals aside, Smith deserves credit for his vision, strength, explosiveness, and understanding of how to follow his massive linemen.

# Corey Miller

## Linebacker

*Teams: New York Giants, 1991–97; Minnesota Vikings, 1999*
*His View: In 1993, Smith turned in one of the toughest performances in NFL history when his team needed it the most—the final game of the season, with the NFC East title on the line. After separating his right shoulder on the rock-hard turf early in the game, Smith came back to finish with 32 carries for 168 yards, and 10 catches for 61 yards and a touchdown. If you watch highlights, you can see Miller, No. 57, making several tackles.*

**W**E THOUGHT THAT we had knocked him out of the game and felt good about that—felt good about making them more one-dimensional. But, he ran back onto the field, and it was amazing what he did.

We had the number-one defense. We were a prideful defense. That was Lawrence Taylor's last year. We were at home, and there was no way Dallas was going to beat us. And to lose, to have a guy with one arm, basically, do what he did and go right through the middle of our defense—one time without even being touched—it was heartbreaking.

It was the greatest memory, having that challenge of playing against one of the greatest teams ever and making some really good plays. But it was also my worst memory because I thought finally we had built that team and had a Super Bowl team. That game is one of the greats that I always talk about. It was one of those games that I'm forced to watch when they show the classics, and all the time people remind me of it.

Emmitt knew how to make explosive moves at the right time. He didn't waste any moves. He set up his blockers very nicely. And he was a tough runner. He wasn't a big physical presence, but his lower body and leg strength were always going for positive yards. He just did a great job of running between the tackles.

That initial contact was tough, and it was tough to get him down because he had great leg drive. When you look back at Emmitt, you think about great vision, knowing when to make that right cut, sticking that foot in the ground, and getting up the field quick. That's what impressed me most about him.

There were a lot of plays where they'd kick out with the fullback and pull the guard. They did not care about tricking you. They lined up and said: "You know what? We're better than you. We're going to out-physical you, and we'll win the game in the fourth quarter." They'd wear you down.

Emmitt was not going to be Barry Sanders. He was not going to wow you by making people miss, or using quick moves or stopping and starting, or highlight reel moves. He wasn't that guy. This debate goes on all the time: Who's the greatest back? Now, if you're to ask me who's the toughest to tackle, I would give you a different answer; I would say Barry Sanders. But when you think about how Emmitt ran behind that offensive line, he was one of the smartest running backs and had the best vision of anyone I ever played with.

## Mark Collins

### Cornerback

**Teams:** *New York Giants, 1986–93; Kansas City Chiefs, 1994–96; Green Bay Packers, 1997; Seattle Seahawks, 1998*
**His View:** *It seemed to Collins there wasn't anything different about one-shouldered Emmitt once he had the ball in his hands.*

**H**E SEEMED LIKE old Emmitt to me. Emmitt still ran the ball like Emmitt. You couldn't tell he was hurt. We couldn't stop

Emmitt when he had two good shoulders, and we couldn't stop him with one.

Now, when he got back up, he got up a little slower, but by the time he got back to the huddle and broke the huddle for the next play, Emmitt was back to being Emmitt. It just showed you how much of a competitor he is, about his determination and will to compete to help his team beat the Giants to go forward. That's a testament to him.

Greg Jackson got him good when he hurt his shoulder, but usually there were no clean shots like that on him—*pow*, knock him backward. You never totally got a clean shot at him. He ran low to the ground, but he ran smart. Anybody who tried to take a kill shot at him, who tried to knock him out of the game or knock him out, those guys were witnesses when Emmitt was running for a long touchdown.

That whole game was a great game. We had our chances, and it went back and forth. You could see the Dallas Cowboys ascending to even greater heights, and the rest of the division going horizontal or down. From that game going forward, us old guys on the field, me and Lawrence Taylor, we knew it. That was it for us. If we would have won the NFC East, I don't think we would have went far in the playoffs anyway. We didn't have the horses, like we used to. But for the Cowboys, it was their time.

# Jessie Tuggle

## Linebacker

**Team:** *Atlanta Falcons, 1987–2000*
**His View:** *Tuggle was the NFL's leading active tackler when he retired, so he had a few tricks for stopping running backs. They didn't always work against Smith, though, who had several big games against Atlanta.*

**I** **PRIDE MYSELF ON** being a big hitter. But I remember him seeming like he had eyes on the side of his head. He just had a feel for when someone was about to hit him or tackle him. You could never seem to get a real hard hit on him.

I didn't rest well when we were going to play the Cowboys. First of all, I knew I had to fight the best offensive line in the league, and then they had the best back in the league. And he's the type of guy who was going to get his 100 yards and get over the goal line with the ball. If you didn't really form tackle him, wrap him up, and run through him, then you were not going to knock him down. The way they tackle now, where they put their shoulder into a guy and hit him real hard and expect him to fall, Emmitt is not the type of back who would go down there.

I recall a game in Atlanta when they gave Emmitt the ball on third-and-short. Because I'd been watching a lot of film, I knew what kind of plays they liked to run. So I came up hard and hit him in the backfield. I hit him almost square in the chest with one of those power hits that knocked down most guys. Then Eugene Robinson hit him at an awkward angle that knocked me away. Somehow, Emmitt got his balance and ran for a touchdown. I'm looking at that tape and thinking, "How in the world did he stay up?"

Emmitt was not a 4.4 guy. He was not a 230-pound back. He was a back who ran with great instinct, which is something you can't teach. Although he wasn't the fastest, he was the best. Emmitt and Moose were the most feared backfield. I had some good hits on both.

I remember one time when we were about to play the Cowboys, Emmitt said something like: "Hey, don't underestimate Jessie Tuggle. This guy's a hard hitter." At that time, he was a superstar. When the best back in the league says something about a linebacker, that meant a lot to me.

When I talk to people about Emmitt, somehow they always bring up Barry Sanders. And I always tell them: These are two totally different backs. Their style of play is totally different. I have a lot of respect for both. I feared both because I knew my work was cut out for me. I feared Barry because he could make me look stupid. If you weren't in the right position, he was going to make you look silly on tape because he was so quick and so elusive. Playing against Emmitt, I knew that if I didn't hit him with everything I had—do what we call "hit and wrap," and bring my hips and legs and drive to him—he was going to make me look bad. He wasn't going to go down to arm tackles.

# Brentson Buckner

## Defensive Lineman

*Teams: Pittsburgh Steelers, 1994–96; Cincinnati Bengals, 1997; San Francisco 49ers, 1998–2000; Carolina Panthers, 2001–05*
*His View: The Steelers managed to slow Smith in the Super Bowl, holding him to 49 yards on 18 carries. Yet Smith still scored twice on short runs after a pair of Larry Brown interceptions put Dallas in the red zone.*

**Y**OU CAN LOOK in his eyes and tell the only answer he wanted was those six points. He ran great all the time, but inside that 5-yard line, it almost became a personal challenge. You have no question when it's close that it's coming to Emmitt. Their best offensive play, especially when they get closer to the end zone, was to turn around and hand it to Emmitt Smith.

But they always had an answer that kept you off balance. When you look at the first touchdown in the Super Bowl, we knew it was coming to Emmitt. We loaded up for it, and they play actioned it and threw it to Jay Novacek for the touchdown.

Emmitt's last touchdown, after the fourth-quarter interception, it was deflating. We felt like we were doing so good, and then—*pow*, they're back on the 6-yard line. It was terrible because we actually had stolen the momentum. We had them. But then, like champions do, they came up with a play when they needed it.

They were going to stick with the run. Their whole thing was: We're good at what we do. We're going to line up and run what we run. You stop it. And if you stop it once, you have to stop it 10 times. They never changed. They ran the same runs. They just kept on coming.

Emmitt had built-in leverage and he used it down there close to the end zone. He ran low to the ground, which maximized his power and cutting ability. He was good at driving his legs. And once you get off the block of one of those big offensive linemen, then you got him coming downhill full speed; that's a lot to ask of a defender.

We knew going into the game that Emmitt was the key. What we tried to do was line up and move around so we weren't going to be where we first lined up when the ball snapped. We just wanted to move and catch them off guard. We tried to do a lot of things to disrupt their running games. We did a good enough job against Emmitt to give us a chance to win.

We knew we had our work cut out for us from their first running play of the game. We knew it was going to be power to their left. We were loaded up on the defense and we're like, "OK we got this stopped." And next thing you know, Emmitt is running down the field for 23 yards because they just blocked it so perfectly. The strong safety had to make a touchdown-saving tackle on the first run of the game. We watched them on film, we knew they were good, but to see it in person you had a greater respect for them.

# Eric Allen

## Cornerback

*Teams: Philadelphia Eagles, 1988–94; New Orleans Saints, 1995–97; Oakland Raiders, 1998–2001*

*His View: A lot of defenders have that nightmare image of Smith running downhill behind giant linemen, but Allen remembers a whole lot of other ways he could hurt a defense.*

**H**E COULD BUST off a 20-yarder or put his head in there and get the fourth-and-1. He didn't really take a lot of hits. He was really crafty. Emmitt was very patient, had really good vision, and just had a nice balance to him when he was running. He'd get into a hole and juke a little bit, then find the perfect spot to burst out. He was tough, too. He'd drop his shoulder at times. He was everything you wanted. He was just perfect for their offense.

At that time, people were in awe of Barry Sanders because he had the moves, but Emmitt was a more complex running back. He had other aspects of his game that helped the Cowboys. Barry, he would take a 12-yard loss to try to make a guy miss. Emmitt wouldn't do that. Emmitt would be patient and always found a way to fall forward or spin forward.

Emmitt was emotional, a great competitor, fiery, had a great respect for the game. But Emmitt would talk to you. So after a play, you could say something to him, good or bad. He broke one time and I caught him, and he said, "You'll never catch me again." A year later, I'm trying to catch him, and at the last minute he shifts his body and I end up whiffing and he ends up scoring. So he was a man of his word, and he didn't let me catch him again.

I remember that Emmitt and Andre Waters did not get along. They were both from Florida and Andre always thought Emmitt got all the credit and didn't deserve it. Whenever we were playing when Andre was there, we'd look for opportunities to tackle him and hold him so Andre could get him.

Emmitt was just this great humble guy, and really didn't understand how someone would dislike him. So before the game, or in the first couple series, I'd say: "Hey, Emmitt, stay away from Andre today. I don't know what happened or what's going on, but dude, he is upset at you."

And for the next two or three plays, he'd be like, "Hey E.A., what did I do?" We're in the middle of the game, and he's talking about why our star safety is mad at him. This would kind of go on, and Andre would play it up, too: "Emmitt, I'm gonna get you."

## Eric Hill

### Linebacker

**Teams:** *Phoenix/Arizona Cardinals, 1989–97; St. Louis Rams, 1998; San Diego Chargers, 1999*
**His View:** *Hill faced Smith plenty in college, when he was at LSU and Smith was at Florida, so he was well aware of the problems Smith presented when they met up in the pros.*

I DON'T THINK PEOPLE give Emmitt enough credit. He wasn't the fastest guy in the world, wasn't the biggest guy in the world. But he had that one step that he would give it and next thing you know you were left standing there. That one step would give him separation from anybody else. He didn't have Barry Sanders speed, but he could separate from his defender all the time.

My biggest problem with Emmitt was, I never wanted to find myself in the open field. There was this little flare route where Emmitt would come out of the backfield. They didn't throw the ball to Emmitt a lot, but it seemed like every time I had him, or every time I was in that zone, they'd throw it to him. And that was my biggest nightmare. You talk about a guy who was scared to death. And he would get me every time.

# Mark Kelso

## Safety

*Team: Buffalo Bills, 1986–93*
*His View: Four weeks after Smith's heroic game against the Giants, the Cowboys played their second straight Super Bowl against the Bills. The Bills led at halftime before Smith poured on his MVP-winning performance: 92 of his 132 yards came after halftime, including 61 of Dallas' 64 yards on the Cowboys' first drive of the third quarter.*

EMMITT DIDN'T SEEM any different to us after halftime. We didn't give up any big runs, but you had a bunch of short runs and kept moving the chains. Sometimes it's the little things, that if they execute better they're going to have success. They just decided they were going to run the ball and were effective doing it. And they just continued to do it.

Then they went on that Emmitt drive where almost every single one was a running play. Emmitt was running hard and they were able to push the pile and control the line of scrimmage. Then it's the same thing for us: "How did that happen?" We realized we kind of had it in the palm of our hands, and it was our opportunity just to clench our fist and finish the deal.

# Charles Mann

## Defensive End

*Teams: Washington Redskins, 1983–93; San Francisco 49ers, 1994*
*His View: Smith scored the first of his NFL-record 164 rushing touchdowns against Washington in 1990, one of many times Mann failed to land a good hit on him.*

**I WANTED TO TEAR** him up, but he would always kind of slither off. You never got a really good shot on him, and that's an art unto itself. I'm telling you, I can't recall one. I challenge anybody to find where he took a really good pop.

You look at Marshawn Lynch. He takes shots all over the place. Emmitt played as long as he did because he never took a bunch of those big hits. He just picked you apart. He'd run to the right, run to the left.

He was frustrating. Sometimes, he would just go down after he did what he had to do—instead of fighting for extra yards and having you strip the ball. It was just, "You know what? I got all I'm going to get here." He wasn't weak or soft or anything like that. He didn't run out of bounds or anything like that. He was just a smart football player. Why take all this unnecessary beating?

# Jason Sehorn

## Cornerback

*Teams: New York Giants, 1994–2002; St. Louis Rams, 2003*
*His View: Smith didn't pile up yards simply because he had the good fortune of running behind a great offensive line. He knew exactly how to use that line.*

**Y**OU'D SEE THOSE road graters coming at you, with him behind them; then he'd make that cut and just pop out of there. Emmitt would disappear back there behind them. A lot of running backs do that, but what separated him and why he was great was that he knew when the hole opened and what to do with it.

All of a sudden he would see a spot and explode. Based on history and running behind that line and their plays, Emmitt had an idea of, "All right, this is where the seam is going to be."

Teams sometimes abandon what they're doing. But the Cowboys never did. Emmitt was always going to run; he was always going to get his 25 or so carries per game. They were going to impose their will, and it just kept coming at you.

# Byron Evans

## Linebacker

*Team: Philadelphia Eagles, 1987–94*
*His View: The Eagles took great pride in holding Smith under 100 yards the first five times they played him, but in 1993 Smith shattered the Cowboys' single-game rushing record against them with 237 yards.*

**I**T WAS THE end of the second quarter and Troy Aikman takes off straight up the middle and he ends up sliding. As he slides, I go over the top of him and I landed on my right forearm and broke it, because I was trying to take Troy Aikman's head off.

In the third quarter they wrapped my arm up. They said, "You know you have a broken arm." I said, "Yeah, I know I got a broken arm, but my team needs me," and I went back out there. That's a rivalry, so by any means necessary.

We knew what they were going to do and we knew what we had to do to stop him. We knew we had to take away Emmitt Smith. On that last score in the fourth quarter, his 62-yard run, Moose Johnston was leading on me. But I couldn't take him on because my arm was broken.

When you were playing America's Team, you always had a chip on your shoulder. To play against the Cowboys, it was a rivalry unlike no other. It never entered my mind to go out of the game because when the rivalry game comes about, you don't go out. We played football, and football is what you played until they had to carry you out.

## Troy Vincent

### Defensive Back

*Teams: Miami Dolphins, 1992–95; Philadelphia Eagles, 1996–2003; Buffalo Bills, 2004–06; Washington Redskins, 2006*
*His View: Everybody knew Smith wasn't the speediest or most powerful back, but defenders paid the price when they started to assume he couldn't do certain things.*

**H**E WASN'T EXTREMELY fast, but fast enough. Wasn't extremely quick, but quick enough. He wasn't a power runner, but had just enough power to run you over. He wasn't great at one thing, but he was good at a whole lot of things.

Emmitt wasn't an easy tackle. He was one that you had to wrap up or he was going to run through your tackle. He had just enough quickness and elusiveness to come out of those tight holes.

Just when you think he's not the Marshall Faulk, or he's not this and not that, well then the next thing you know, you're chasing him into the end zone. Our defensive coaches used to say: "If you break down in your technique or you don't hold this gap, you're going to be watching 22 go into the end zone."

# CHAPTER 15

# FACING THE BIG, MEAN, NASTY LINE

**T**HE COWBOYS OFFENSIVE line of the 1990s was gigantic and terrifying. That's a sentiment from their peers—themselves large men who made a living being terrifying. Most of the time Dallas had four starters well over 300 pounds at a time when that milestone wasn't always a given. In addition to being big and scary, these linemen were very good. They were smart, quick, and strong—Larry Allen could bench-press 700 pounds. The combination of those skills gave Emmitt Smith gaping holes to run through and Troy Aikman all sorts of time to find Michael Irvin. In other words, the line made The Triplets into stars. If the blockers were considered a single unit, the Dallas offense of the 1990s might more accurately be known as The Quadruplets. The cast rotated some, but the mainstays were Allen, Erik Williams, Nate Newton, Mark Tuinei, and Mark Stepnoski. Other key members were Kevin Gogan, John Gesek, Derek Kennard, and Ray Donaldson. Pro Bowls were regular stops for many, but the most decorated of them all was Allen, who arrived in Dallas after the first two Super Bowls. He went into the Pro Football Hall of Fame in 2013 and the Dallas Cowboys Ring of Honor in 2011. He was on the NFL's All-Decade Team for the 1990s and 2000s.

# Eric Hill

## Linebacker

*Teams: Phoenix/Arizona Cardinals, 1989–97; St. Louis Rams, 1998; San Diego Chargers, 1999*
*His View: Hill got a double dose of the Dallas linemen every year as a divisional rival. None were fun to face, but there was one guy he especially dreaded.*

LARRY ALLEN IS the toughest offensive lineman I played against. I prided myself on being a physical player, but ask any middle linebacker in that era and they'll tell you that Larry Allen was a problem child nobody wanted to deal with.

One time I went at Larry Allen so hard, and I thought I really got him. It was a collision and everybody heard it. We got back to the huddle and I was like, "Man, I knocked the shit out of Big Allen." Everybody was looking at me, and they were like, "But you got the worst end of the lick." I was like, "What are you talking about?" And they said, "Man, that dude bent your damn helmet."

That's when I looked down and realized that blood was trickling down my nose. He had bent the center of my facemask, and it broke my nose. The hinges on the side of the helmet had been busted. So the thing was flying up and down. I went to the sideline after that and I had to get a new facemask.

Larry's not a talker. He didn't say a lot. He just kicked your ass and kept moving. So I tried to get in his head, get him talking, get him off his game a little bit.

They used to run this little trap draw play, where the center blocks back, and the guard comes around right over the middle linebacker. As a linebacker, you had to time that play perfectly. You had to guess, then blitz it and catch Larry before he could turn those shoulders and hit him in the hole, and you can just create a big pile. Well, they ran that trap play and I saw it. I guessed it and I hit it dead on. I caught Larry before he could turn those shoulders, got under his pads, knocked him back a little bit, and hit Emmitt for no gain. Of course, I'm jumping up. I'm like, "You better not bring more than that!" I'm all over the place and I'm excited. Three plays later, they run the same play. This time, I didn't blitz and I guessed wrong. Boy, Larry Allen came around in that hole, and he hit me, and I'm telling you, by the time I hit the ground, I was probably about five yards back. And that was the first time I ever heard Larry talk. Larry's standing over me, yelling, "Fill that shit up Hill, fill that shit up," meaning fill the hole we collided in. All I could do was shake my head.

## Brentson Buckner

### Defensive Lineman

**Teams:** *Pittsburgh Steelers, 1994–96; Cincinnati Bengals, 1997; San Francisco 49ers, 1998–2000; Carolina Panthers, 2001–05*
**His View:** *Facing Allen was painful. Facing Williams was painful. Pittsburgh's 3–4 defense meant Buckner spent most of the Super Bowl fighting off both Williams and Allen.*

**T**HAT WAS LIKE a war. It wasn't one guy coming then another guy. They hit you with the blunt force of 700 pounds at the same time. That was probably the sorest I've been after the game, because their whole thing was about being physical, play-in and play-out. After the game, my hands hurt, my neck hurt, everything hurt— wrist, back, knee. You're just sore all over because you just had a true football game against true football players. It was a full day's work, a full-body-type exercise.

Erik Williams used to have this thing we used to call the head-butt technique. When we were pass-rushing, if he could grab you he would just snatch you and pull you to him and head-butt you as hard as he could, right in the middle of your face mask. Guys would come back to the huddle and you could see their eyes roll back in their head. Or, if you went in and had your head down, he would just club you in the back of your neck.

He played the game the way it was supposed to be played. There wasn't a play off. There wasn't anything he wouldn't do up until the whistle. Erik Williams was just pretty nasty. I think he was a year removed from a car accident, so people would say he had lost a step, but he was still at the top of the NFL.

Larry Allen was a big, physical, strong guy who was made for the run game. Larry always looked like he was mad at the world. Before the snap you could look at his fingers and you could see all the blood going out of his hand because he had all his weight forward. You knew he was coming off the ball. And when he came off, and being a guy who could bench 700 pounds, you had your hands full.

Those two guys, that was probably one of the best guard-tackle combinations I faced in my entire career.

# Na'il Diggs

## Linebacker

*Teams: Green Bay Packers, 2000–05; Carolina Panthers, 2006–09; St. Louis Rams, 2010; San Diego Chargers, 2011*
*His View: Diggs, like many other players—and it's probably safe to say all players—wanted no part of Allen.*

**W**HAT WAS IT like facing Larry Allen? It was a subtle fear of another human being. You always had to know where he was. It was more of an avoidance-type thing, kind of like a skill player you always wanted to account for. As the play goes, you don't really want to run into him. It was respect, but it was a very conscious, subtle fear of running into that man. You see him punishing too many guys. You don't want to be that guy on film who everyone sees getting punished by him.

For the years that I played against him, it was hard because they had a lot of other big men on that line. You had to worry about the other guys coming off on you. And one thing you could count on was the Dallas Cowboys would punish you.

Other offensive linemen, sometimes they'd cut your knees out. That was one thing you never had to worry about Dallas week. They were just going to hit you. It was almost like a statement. They were saying: You know what? We're just going to get the biggest men in the world, the best athletic-wise, and we're going to put them on our team. And we're going to make you tackle behind those big guys. We're going to make your big guys face our big guys.

My words can't really do it justice or paint a picture of what it was really like when you're on the field and standing across from these guys, when you're standing five yards away from these dudes and knowing you're in the most violent of arenas, with these huge human beings on the opposite team you're on, and they're twice your size.

With Larry, it was like when I played with Orlando Pace at Ohio State: Once he got his hands on you, it was a done deal. You were done. It looked like a grown man just playing with a teenage son, throwing him on the ground, with moderate effort. It was just a mismatch, a laws-of-physics mismatch.

# Charles Haley

## Hall of Fame Defensive End/Outside Linebacker

*Teams:* San Francisco 49ers, 1986–91; 1998–99; Dallas Cowboys, 1992–96

*His View:* Haley had a unique view of the line. He played against many of them during his years in San Francisco, then also faced them as a teammate in Dallas.

**T**HEY WERE GREAT, even in practice. We didn't go in pads in practice with Bill Walsh in San Francisco, but that was Coach Jimmy Johnson's style of play: Everything was full speed.

I called Mark Tuinei "The Dancing Bear" because he tried to dance with me when I went against him. Erik Williams, man, he was just solid. He'd try that one punch. He'd get you with that one punch, and it was game time. It was off of your first step. He'd give you a chest punch, or in the face. Man, he was nasty. He tried to hit you on every play, so you had to be prepared for it. I practiced mobility, not power on the guy. It was practice, but it was pretty much the same as a game. I tried not to go over there very often.

Big Nate, he'd just try to lean on you. Larry Allen was a rookie my last year there, and you could see the potential in him. He could play any position. And when he played it, he played it well. And Stepnoski, he was a physical specimen. He was so short and so light, but nobody could run over him. He guided that ship any way he wanted.

For me, in order to get better, you have to go against the best. I got to do that week in and week out with the Cowboys, because that big offensive line was great.

# Corey Miller

## Linebacker

*Teams:* New York Giants, 1991–97; Minnesota Vikings, 1999
*His View:* Among Miller's many unpleasant memories against the Cowboys line was getting jammed in the face mask by Williams—a tactic the NFL has since banned in what's widely known as the "Erik Williams Rule."

THE GUY I absolutely hated to play was Erik Williams. He was going to be nasty. He was going to go hands to the face mask. If they called those penalties for that back then, he'd probably be out of the game, because he was always quick to get you with the hands to the face. Every time we'd play them, I knew, you better bring your "A Game" and you better bring your "Mean Game." We always would fight and scrap and push and shove after the play. But I respected him because of his toughness. I think he's one of the best to ever play that position. He was great with fundamentals, but he had that nastiness of a linebacker.

The scariest guy, though, could have been Larry Allen. I hated him because of his power and his speed. To be 325 and to run the way he ran, and the muscles on top of it all. He was a scary-looking dude, with that big old head and the face mask. When he pulled, I used to have some crazy collisions with him. You dreaded that. I don't think I've ever played against a player as strong as him. He scared me more than anybody. I wasn't going to take that all day long, so I would start cutting him, hitting him around his knees and trying to cause a big pile. You can't go against a man like that 30 times a game without wearing out your shoulders and neck. I was in the ice tub for a day or two after playing them.

# Gilbert Brown

## Nose Tackle

*Team:* Green Bay Packers, 1993–2003
*His View:* Anchoring the middle of a 3–4 defense, Brown wound up battling all three of Dallas' interior linemen: Allen, Newton, and Stepnoski.

**I**'M GOING TO tell it till the day I die: It always starts up front, no matter what you do. You can have Mickey Mouse back there at quarterback and Daffy Duck at tailback. If you've got a strong offensive line in front of them, you win the game, period.

Getting ready for the Cowboys was different because they had everybody. You take away the run, here comes the pass. You take away the pass, here comes the run. And they had big hogs who could make it all happen. They had two factors that nobody else had: Those two guards, Larry Allen and Nate Newton. Both Larry Allen and Nate Newton were strong, both of them moved well for their size, and both left an impression on you. You would always say about lines that the left side is weaker or the right side is weaker, but both sides were strong.

They were really the cornerstone of that offense. Those two guys right there set the tone. And Stepnoski, that little son of a bitch, he was fast as hell. I could be standing there and he's on my right, then all of a sudden I'm like, "Dog, how'd you end up over there?" It wasn't that he put fear in anybody, but you knew that this guy was going to be where he was supposed to be. He's going to be technique-sound, and he's got the help with Nate and Larry to move your ass out of there.

But Larry Allen was a guy who stands alone. When you're playing a game it's not like a normal double team with Larry. You could feel Larry coming down on you. With other guys, you couldn't even feel them. Larry was so strong and so powerful that you could feel him. Nate was good at moving the crowd as well, but Larry just had more power. It's rare to see two guys so strong on the double team.

Larry, you could tell he was a no-nonsense, no-jokes kind of guy. He was going to go out there, do his job, hit you in the mouth if he had to, and go about his business. Nate got mouthy. Me and Nate used to always go back and forth a little bit out there. He always said he was prettier than me or thought that he was skinnier than me. So we'd get out there and we'd do a little shouting match back and forth. Nate's going to let you know. He's going to joke on you, you're going to joke on him, we're going to have a little fun about it. He was a fat, funny, jovial guy. I like him. Some guys get out there they start talking that stuff, "I'm going to do this to you and that to you," but you don't pay them no attention. It's cool sometimes to be able to have a little banter back and forth but knowing we're doing our job at the same time. If I gotta take your head off, I'm going to do it. If you gotta take my head off, you'd do the same to me.

I liked playing against Nate and Larry because it made you better. When you had two big powerful lines going together, like when Green Bay was playing Dallas, it's one of those things where only the strong survive. These guys, each and every one of them, they had a killer instinct and they came out to play. And they wanted to show you how good they were.

# Eric Allen

## Cornerback

**Teams:** *Philadelphia Eagles, 1988–94; New Orleans Saints, 1995–97; Oakland Raiders, 1998–2001*
**His View:** *Allen remembers a game when a defensive end did something he's never seen before in the NFL, due to a beating by Williams.*

**T**HE ONLY CONVERSATION I had with them was one game when we had this defensive end who was talking about Erik from over on the other side. This defensive end is consistently talking, talking, talking. And Erik was like: "Hey E.A., what's this dude talking about? If he wants to talk, have him come over here on my side."

The defensive end didn't come over, so Erik took it out on the defensive end who was on his side. He was just throwing him around like a rag doll. They were running the ball on us and beating us down, and Erik was throwing this defensive end all over the ground.

They had run the ball for like 50 yards. They were on our 20, going in. I see our defensive end 10 yards downfield on one knee. I was like: "What the heck is going on? Do we need a timeout? Is he hurt or what?" So he starts walking off the field toward our sideline. It's a timeout, so I run over and I'm like, "What are you doing?" He was like, "I quit." I said, "Excuse me?" He said: "I quit. I can't do this."

Big Erik had made this professional football player walk off the field, completely walk off the field, in the middle of a game. I can't recall if he came back. It was just unbelievable that a grown man walked off the football field. That's the kind of dominance that line was about.

They were grown men, and you didn't mess around with those dudes. They were like giants. I stayed away from them. You could get hurt messing with Big Erik and Nate and all those dudes. There was no way I was about to put my head up in there.

# Aeneas Williams

## Hall of Fame Cornerback

*Teams:* *Phoenix/Arizona Cardinals, 1991–2000; St. Louis Rams, 2001–04*
*His View:* *Aeneas Williams also remembers Erik Williams prompting defensive linemen to reconsider their career choice.*

**W**ATCHING FILM, I promise you, I've seen Erik Williams make All-Pro players quit because of his tenacity, and with that head-butt he used to do.

I remember he also used to call Simeon Rice out. At that time, Simeon would have the flexibility to go left or right. He'd come up to the line and say, "Simeon, come over here," and he'd say it in words I wouldn't say.

There was a nastiness about that line. I played against a lot of great offensive linemen, but I don't know if I came across guys who were talented, physical, and also just outright nasty like an Erik Williams.

## Clyde Simmons

### Defensive End

*Teams: Philadelphia Eagles, 1986–93; Arizona Cardinals, 1994–95; Jacksonville Jaguars, 1996–97; Cincinnati Bengals, 1998; Chicago Bears, 1999–2000*

*His View: The darkest day for the Cowboys' great offensive line came in 1991, when the offense didn't score a point and they allowed 11 sacks to the Eagles. Simmons led the way with four and a half sacks.*

**I** HAD MARK TUINEI'S number that day. There were good days and there were bad days with him; it just depended on which day it was. He was always a good player, but some days it was easier to see what he was doing to try to block me.

In the early years, Mark wasn't as big as he got to be. He was a pretty good athlete, but then his weight got pretty high and that's when I was able to take advantage of him with athleticism. But, at the same time, when he got bigger it could also be a problem for me. As he got bigger and stronger, I had to get really physical to get his hands off me. It made it a little more of uphill sledding for me.

The thing I always admired about him is he was always competing, every play. For the most part the games were clean and hard, but every now and then he would do something that would piss me off a little bit and we'd have our words. Like once he stepped on my hand, and I knew he did it intentionally. It was that four-and-a-half-sack day, and so I just rabbit-punched him in his thigh, just to let him know he couldn't get away with that. Then he'd get back to playing more clean football, none of those cheap-shot tactics.

I also remember this fight I was having with Nate Newton. It was a huge fight. If I remember correctly, somebody hit Troy Aikman just after or just before the whistle on a dead ball or something. They took offense to it and one thing led to another. There was pushing, and next thing you know, it's a brawl. We were under the pile, me and Nate; both of us had each other's hands. We were under that pile looking each other right in the face. We were saying, "If you hit me, I swear I'm going to kick you in your nuts." It probably felt like we were under there all day, but it was probably 10–15 seconds.

# Jessie Tuggle

## Linebacker

*Team: Atlanta Falcons, 1987–2000*
*His View: Tuggle usually came out on the better end of any collision, but not when Allen was involved—especially on national TV.*

**I PLAYED AT ABOUT** 220 pounds, but I was extremely strong. I had a 500-pound bench press and I was quick, so my power angles were really good as far as taking on big guys. Normally, I'm lower and I'm stronger. They may be bigger, but I'm stronger.

But Larry Allen was way bigger than me and stronger than me. And if you lined us up in a 40-yard dash, he could probably outrun me even though he was 325 pounds. A true freak of nature.

One time we were playing them and John Madden was commentating on TV. I recall a play where I'm coming up and trying to brace myself and getting in great position to get Emmitt, and Larry comes around and hits me face to face. He caught me between steps. So right before I put my left foot down, it's like three inches from the ground, and Larry hits me so hard that it literally knocked me on my back. I was called The Hammer back in the day. I never got knocked on my back, ever. But, eventually it happens to the best of us.

It wouldn't have been that bad, except John Madden kept yelling something like: "Let's see that play one more time! All-Pro linebacker Jessie Tuggle gets hit by Larry Allen! Let's look at that in slow motion!" And I'm totally getting pancaked. This was before his first Pro Bowl, I think. He wasn't as well known. It was unbelievable.

# Willie Roaf

## Hall of Fame Tackle

**Teams:** *New Orleans Saints, 1993–2001; Kansas City Chiefs, 2002–05*
**His View:** *Roaf never played for the Cowboys, but he felt like it once a year when he went to the Pro Bowl. There he found that many, if not most, line mates were from Dallas.*

IT WOULD BE Tuinei, Erik, Larry, Nate, or Stepnoski. There'd always be two or three Cowboy linemen in the Pro Bowl. I really respected those guys. That was probably one of the top five lines that played together. It was a pleasure watching them play.

I always looked up to Mark Tuinei because he was kind of like me: real quick feet and real good hands, a leaner offensive lineman. I was a young guy wanting some advice.

I remember being at the Pro Bowl and talking to Mark and asking him what it took to play in the league a long time. Mark just told me to take care of myself.

# Jason Sehorn

## Cornerback

*Teams: New York Giants, 1994–2002; St. Louis Rams, 2003*
*His View: When he was drafted out of Sonoma State, Allen immediately looked like a man among boys in the NFL. Imagine what he looked like before Sonoma State, when he faced junior college competition. Sehorn saw it happen when he was at Shasta College facing Allen's Butte College team.*

**H**E JUST DIDN'T belong there. Here's what it looked like: Imagine you're watching a Pop Warner football game, and a high school kid is playing tackle. He was just so much bigger and so much more gifted size-wise.

They should not have let him play. You know how they do with Pop Warner kids, if you get too big you can't play? They should have done that with Larry Allen in junior college. He should not have been able to play with those guys because he was hurting people.

I think their running back went on to get a full-ride scholarship. Basically he went behind Larry Allen for two years and put up huge numbers. It was all Larry Allen.

Larry Allen was by far the nastiest individual I've ever played against. He was just a beast. In Dallas you'd have them coming around the end and, I mean, good luck. Larry Allen was the most agile. And he was just a house. Their tackles were beasts as well. And they all moved. They pulled a lot.

I see today, so many of these offensive linemen get out in the open, and they're just there, or they whiff on a guy or they miss. It seemed like the Cowboys never missed. When those guys got out in the open and were supposed to hit the linebacker or the corner or the safety, they got them.

## Charles Mann

### Defensive End

*Teams: Washington Redskins, 1983–93; San Francisco 49ers, 1994*
*His View: Mann remembers briefly being a teammate with Newton, who signed as a free agent in Washington in 1983 but didn't make the team. He squared off against both Williams and Newton, who spent a couple years at tackle.*

IN 1983, NATE was like 295 pounds. Now, we fast-forward about 10 years, Nate Newton is like 365 and a mainstay on the line for the Cowboys. Getting around him was not an easy task. In fact, you didn't get around him and you couldn't go through him. You hoped Troy Aikman would hold the ball long enough that you might be able to jump and tip the ball or something. I got my share of sacks, but I tell you, it was really hard because of Nate.

The next offensive lineman that owned that spot was Erik Williams. Erik was a beast; I have to give the brother his due. He was the most angry offensive lineman I've ever seen. He was vicious. If I happened to fall down, I tried to roll out of the way, because he would just spear you on the ground.

Against the run I was fine with him, but against the pass he was the nastiest offensive lineman I ever faced. I would put him in the same mention as Jackie Slater, who played 20 years and is a Hall of Famer with the Rams. You were live even a little bit past the whistle with Erik. If you got to the tackle and you weren't the first one there or the second or the third, and you tried to jump on the pile, or you didn't jump on the pile but stopped short, well, you now got crushed by Erik as he came over to spear you out of the way. So, he would knife you in the back when you were lying on the ground, and if you stood over a pile, he took you out, which is very embarrassing when you're watching your film study. You're looking with your peers, and they're laughing because you got KO'd standing over the pile.

He was just nasty. I don't know if he'll have a chance of making the Hall of Fame, but he would have my vote.

# CHAPTER 16

# FACING THE RING COLLECTORS

---

Charles Haley
Defensive End (1992–96), No. 94
Pro Football Hall of Fame, Dallas Cowboys Ring of Honor

Deion Sanders
Cornerback (1995–99), No. 21
Pro Football Hall of Fame

**C**HARLES HALEY AND Deion Sanders built stellar careers elsewhere before adding to their Super Bowl ring collections with the Cowboys. Their time in Dallas was short, but their impact was substantial. Haley arrived with two titles from San Francisco and then became the first player in NFL history to earn five rings. Sanders won a title in his only year in San Francisco before signing what was then the richest contract in football to become the Cowboys' shutdown cornerback. Sanders gave the Cowboys a Super Bowl–caliber secondary again, with the side benefit of weakening the San Francisco defense. Sanders picked off 14 passes as a Cowboy, taking two of them back for touchdowns. He also had three punt returns for scores and even lined up as receiver. Haley's speed rush gave the Cowboys a new dimension on the defensive line and lifted them to Super Bowl status. Haley arrived in Dallas averaging about 10 sacks a season, and he brought intensity and a focus on winning (which was all he ever knew in San Francisco).

# FACING CHARLES HALEY

## Jackie Slater
## Hall of Fame Tackle

*Team:* Los Angeles/St. Louis Rams, 1976–95
*His View:* Slater's career spanned the great Dallas defensive ends over three decades, from Ed "Too Tall" Jones to Haley. He recalls Haley being much more than a speed rusher.

CHARLES HALEY BROUGHT to the table an unbelievable amount of momentum and change of direction, and he could counter the mistakes that offensive linemen made. If you went the wrong way, or if you had your weight in the wrong area, he was going to force you to go where you didn't want to go. Then he would counter you. That's the most dangerous type of pass-rusher, the guys who read and anticipate your body movement, then counter. You can't do that unless you're explosively quick. That's what made him special.

He played with great leverage. A lot of people underestimated his strength, but he was strong as well. He had the combination of speed and mass. That's the equation for force: speed times mass. And he had enough speed and mass to generate a powerful impact when he wanted to. That was the thing that made him more dangerous. He'd run over you, then he'd turn around and make you lean, then roll right around you.

I never had much problem with him talking to me. He'd just put his hand on the ground and you'd hear him talking. Then you'd hear him talking to his boys as we broke the huddle. Then he'd get quiet and focused as the ball was snapped. But he was verbal. He was the mouthpiece of most of the efforts of the defenses he played on. He'd just say things and get people going.

I got to meet him when I played with him at the Pro Bowl, and he was a very blunt guy, and a fun guy. He was the type of guy you like to have around, the type of guy you'd like to have on your team. Because you knew there would never be a dull moment when he was around there. I marveled at his athleticism. I was not amazed that championships followed him everywhere he went. If you wanted to have a Super Bowl champion, you needed to have a guy like Charles on your team.

# Randall Cunningham

## Quarterback

**Teams:** *Philadelphia Eagles, 1985–95; Minnesota Vikings, 1997–99; Dallas Cowboys, 2000; Baltimore Ravens, 2001*
**His View:** *Cunningham was sacked three times by Haley in one game in 1994, so he knew just how much Haley could wreck an offense.*

**Y**OU KNOW WHAT I remember about that game? If he was anywhere around the ball, his arms were going to bat the ball down, or he was going to strip me. Whether it was a sack or whether I was trying to get away, it seemed like he would just be at the right place at the right time.

Charles was totally the opposite of Randy White. Always talking, always interjecting, always trying to get you off of your game. He was not a quiet player. He was the kind of guy you just heard all the time. After every play he was complaining to the referees, "These guys were holding me!"

But Charles was an excellent player, the kind of guy you want on your team. He was very disruptive. He would always disrupt the offense with his speed. He was a guy who was a little bit lighter; he wasn't the Reggie White type who was big and powerful and strong. But Charles would do it just based on relentlessness. Whenever he went out for a play or two, I knew it was just to get a breath so he could come in even faster the next play, so that made me try to catch my breath.

# Brent Jones

## Tight End

*Team:* San Francisco 49ers, 1987–97
*His View:* *Jones recalls Haley as a great—albeit sometimes difficult—teammate, and he wonders how different the Dallas-San Francisco rivalry could have been if Haley had never left the 49ers.*

**I REMEMBER THAT RIGHT** when I got to the 49ers, Haley had been there a year and was really kind of at an inflection point in his career, with his speed, his strength, and his knowledge of the defense. He was always a very sophisticated guy on the field. He wasn't a guy who kept doing the wrong thing. He was very bright. He understood the defense.

I'm sure he did this throughout his years, but each year he'd find two or three guys to pick on. Well, he felt like he wanted to pick on me. So I used to have to block him and go against him in practice all the time because I wasn't a starter yet and he was. He wasn't a full-time starter, maybe, but getting lots of playing time. Yeah, lots of pushing, lots of shoving, a few extracurricular blows along the way. I think there was a mutual respect, though.

When we traded him, the Cowboys weren't yet, "the Cowboys" we're talking about now. I can't imagine that if we had known that they were going to have that rapid of an ascension that we would have ever thought about trading him to what was about to become our bitter rivals. And I do believe if Charles Haley had stayed with the 49ers I'd have a couple more Super Bowl rings.

I lined up against him when he was in Dallas more than a handful of times. I'd have to block him. He was pretty tough for his size. The biggest concern with Charles was pass-blocking him. There were very few times I would be on him one-on-one. He was one of the guys where the chip block was used. You'd go by and give the tackle some help, punch a guy or stop him, or stand him up and stop his momentum so the tackle could take him over. His first two steps were just spectacular. He could just explode. He had great hands. He used to work in the off-season doing karate and some of those things.

It was weird facing him for the first time when he was with Dallas. From a run-blocking perspective I was fine. From a pass-blocking perspective, there's a few guys you get that feeling of: "Uh-oh. I better make sure my sets are good. I better make sure I'm helping. I better make sure I know where everybody else is if I'm blocking him one-on-one."

There were only three or four guys over my career where you kind of felt that; Haley was one of them. Lawrence Taylor was one, Kevin Greene was one, for a few years Tim Harris with the Packers, and Derrick Thomas. Those are the guys. I promise you they made our tackles lose sleep the weeks of our games against them.

Charles was a huge trash talker on our team and a huge trash talker in the locker room, and at practice. Almost to the point where sometimes your head would want to explode. Interestingly enough, he didn't say boo as a Cowboy when he played against us—which was pretty disciplined of him. I don't know if it was intentional or if he had just changed, but he didn't say a whole lot, so good for him. We were expecting ranting-and-raving Charles. We never saw that, though. He was just a professional, playing his tail off there. What a huge impact he made for the Cowboys.

Who knows exactly the reason he was traded. Yeah, he talked trash, he used to scream and yell and do stuff, but he was always a hard worker and he always brought it on the field. There were times where he'd drive you crazy and you'd be like, "Yeah, let's get rid of him." And there'd be times when you'd go, "I can't believe we got rid of him."

# Willie Roaf

## Hall of Fame Tackle

*Teams: New Orleans Saints, 1993–2001; Kansas City Chiefs, 2002–05*
*His View: Roaf was a young player and Haley was a renowned pass-rusher when they faced off—Roaf was instantly impressed by his elder.*

**H**E ALWAYS GAVE you all he had. I remember the year he had the back surgery and he still came out there to play for the team with a bad back. He sacrificed his body for the team, and that shows a lot of character.

Charles played with a lot of leverage. He was real shifty. He was one of those guys you had to keep blocking till the end because he was going to keep coming. He had some long arms and relentlessness to try to get to the quarterback. My thing was to keep him from getting upfield.

He used his speed on a lot of guys, and I think the fact that I was getting to a set point and didn't allow him to use his speed, that did frustrate him. I was pretty quick, so a guy who was going to use speed on me and didn't try to bull me a lot, I liked that a lot. I had more problems with a guy who had power.

I remember when we played them on a Monday night game. I was really excited against him and making sure I had a good set on him to avoid trouble. I remember it was a while before I got in my stance. He said he couldn't gauge me because I was shifting around. I just wanted to make sure I cut him off so he couldn't get upfield.

I played in the Pro Bowl with him and kind of got to know him. I just remember him being loud at the Pro Bowl. When he got tired of practice, he would start yelling and stuff. He thought we were practicing too long, and he told the coaches it was time to shut the practice down. When Charles told them to shut it down, they shut it down.

## Mark Bruener

### Tight End

*Teams: Pittsburgh Steelers, 1995–2003; Houston Texans, 2004–08*
*His View: Bruener was a rookie when he drew the assignment of trying to help slow Haley during the Super Bowl.*

**I CAN REMEMBER THE** emphasis on him going into the Super Bowl, because of how powerful and dominant he was and what he was able to do both in the run and the pass game. I remember our game plan was for me to chip him and try to knock him off his initial track with his pass-rush.

His pure strength to me was unique. Charles was athletic. But as far as pure strength goes, if you were trying to move him it was like dead weight. He played with emotion, but I also remember him as a guy who is just lined up across from you doing his work.

At that time everybody was talking about their offensive weapons. However, while their defense may not have had the household name recognition across the board, they were a very, very tough defense.

# Charles Mann
## Defensive End

*Teams: Washington Redskins, 1983–93; San Francisco 49ers, 1994*
*His View: Mann recalls being impressed by Haley's work against Washing-ton's famous Hogs on the offensive line. He also (sometimes) enjoyed Haley's antics during the Pro Bowl.*

**T**YPICALLY I WENT to the sidelines and I got a drink and watched Charles work. It was just fun. We did our battle, so it was our chance to see our line handle their defense. Charles Haley would get to the quarterback faster than anybody. I'd be watching thinking, "Gosh, he's lighter than I am." I was 275. How was he taking Joe Jacoby and pushing him back like that? I'm really glad he's going into the Hall of Fame. He deserves it.

At the Pro Bowl, we almost got in a fight a couple of times because he just got on my nerves. He was always messing around. He was just always playing around. Sometimes it was a time to play, and sometimes it was time to take care of business. At the Pro Bowl, he never took care of business. He just played around. He was practicing with his shoes untied at every practice one year. I said, "Wait till this joker trips over his own shoes." But he never tripped. I didn't understand it.

# FACING DEION SANDERS

## Jerry Rice

### Hall of Fame Receiver

*Teams:* San Francisco 49ers, 1985–2000; Oakland Raiders, 2001–04; Seattle Seahawks, 2004

*His View:* Facing Sanders meant a great challenge physically and mentally. In addition to the speed and everything else, Sanders had a way of distracting his opponents with all sorts of casual chitchat on the field.

REALLY WANTED TO kick his butt, he really wanted to kick my butt, and that's what a rivalry's all about. How can you not get up for Deion Sanders? I don't care which uniform he has on. He really pushed me to work harder because I knew my work was cut out for me whenever I got ready to face him. It was the ultimate challenge because I knew I was going up against the best.

I remember nights before big games, I was up thinking about the opponents I would have during that game and how I would capitalize on them. Even now, we talk about the matchup, and he was doing the same thing—he couldn't sleep. He was up pacing around and thinking about what he had to do to try to contain me. So there was a lot of respect.

You would hear people doing commentary leading up to the game, and the media talking about how Deion Sanders is going up against Jerry Rice and Deion is their shutdown corner. As a receiver, you don't like to hear about a shutdown corner. It's almost like a slap in your face. I was like, "Hey, give me a little bit respect." So that really motivated me to go out and play my best football.

Deion got me many times. I remember one time, I had Deion beat, and I'm just saying: "Throw the ball!" I think it was Steve

Young. And the second he released that ball, Deion accelerated to that ball so fast it was just unbelievable. It was like a blur, and he was able to make the interception. Deion was so deceptive. He'd bait the quarterback into throwing the football; then all of a sudden he has that acceleration.

It's one of those things where you know that this guy is a freak of nature, but you've just got to keep working hard and hopefully wear him down. I always wanted to wear my opponent down. Even on a run play I would sprint 60 or 80 yards downfield and have that guy chasing me and hopefully try to wear him out. And during the fourth quarter I could say, "OK, he's tired now, maybe I can take advantage of him." But with Deion, you had to just continue to work hard.

I've never seen a guy who could be so fast in a split second. He could just explode to that football and catch it. And once he gets that ball, you'd see this guy just run away from everybody. Deion was like a raptor. He didn't have any high-knee action. You look at all the track stars and how they run, they all have that high-knee action. But he just kind of glided along the ground, and nobody could catch him. There are some fast guys in the NFL, but Deion had exceptional speed. It was just like everybody else was standing still, and this guy's doing his dance in the end zone. Deion was a showman, but he was so talented and so gifted that he could back that all up. He would do things out of the ordinary that most defensive backs couldn't do.

We all know Deion is not confrontational. He didn't want to tackle as much. It was so funny because I would try to block him and he would say to me, "Hey, look, Jerry, you don't have to worry about me tackling, OK?" He came straight out and told me that, and I'm looking at him like, "Huh?" He said: "Hey look, just release or run me off or something, because my job is to cover people. That's what I do." So, I just tried to be a little more physical with him at the line of scrimmage.

I don't disrespect anyone on the football field. I'll go out and say hi, but I'm not social because I'm all about the business. I'm ready to go to work, and this is what I take my pride in. I remember one time, right before they snapped the ball, right at the line of scrimmage, Deion wants to shake my hand. The quarterback is calling out the cadence, and Deion is reaching out to shake my hand. So I'm slapping his hand away. He wants to shake my hand and I'm slapping it away, and next thing you know we're doing battle. OK, after we do battle I'll come over and shake your hand and we can talk or whatever, but before that, we're about to get dirty.

Deion always wanted to engage on the football field, He wanted to talk and everything. Like: "Jerry, how you doing? How's everything going?" He wanted to catch up and chitchat a little bit. But you couldn't fall for that. You knew he was going to socialize with you, but when he got the chance he was going to get that interception, and there was going to be no catching him. I think he just wanted you to relax, to let your guard down a little bit.

We made the worst mistake because we traded Charles Haley to the Dallas Cowboys. And then we had Deion leave too, and the media was talking about Deion leaving and made such a big deal out of it. I think that really left a bad taste in my mouth. I knew the rivalry had gotten bigger the second he went to Dallas; I knew it because we hated those Cowboys, and those Cowboys hated us.

# Randall Cunningham

## Quarterback

*Teams:* *Philadelphia Eagles, 1985–95; Minnesota Vikings, 1997–99; Dallas Cowboys, 2000; Baltimore Ravens, 2001*
*His View:* *Cunningham remembered having two choices against Sanders, and both made his life more difficult: Avoid throwing to his side, or try outsmarting him.*

## FACING AMERICA'S TEAM

**I** **REMEMBER WE WERE** playing in Dallas in the playoffs in my last year in Philly, and I threw the ball and it was a *little* behind. And sure enough Deion caught it and man, I had to go tackle him, and he put on one of those little moves with the ball hanging out in the air. Game over.

Deion kept you on your toes. Deion would sit back there right about nine yards, eight yards, and he would not move because he had catch-up speed. So he would sit there and sometimes he'd act like he wasn't looking at you. Deion was a sneaky type of player. Deion would act like he was going to backpedal, but he wouldn't. And if he saw your arm come up, oh, he was charging and you were going to have to make a tackle because he wasn't going to drop an interception.

I wasn't going to throw it his way all the time. I wasn't going to give him the opportunity. Sooner or later he was either going to bat the ball down or pick it off. So I played the percentages and I just wasn't going to go for that. I would just go the other way, even when they had double coverage on the other side. There was a reason he was on an island by himself. He could handle a third of the field.

He and Darrell Green remind me of one another. As a matter of fact, somebody asked me about the number-one defensive back, and those two are neck and neck. They were on a page by themselves.

It was hard knowing Deion was such a great athlete. I didn't know how fast he was, but I knew how flamboyant he was. That flamboyant style, with his speed and his confidence—he was one of the most confident defensive backs I've ever seen. Deion would make you look bad just with his little style things. It was nothing against you; it was just his style of game.

# Ernie Mills

## Wide Receiver

**Teams:** *Pittsburgh Steelers, 1991–96; Carolina Panthers, 1997; Dallas Cowboys, 1998–99*
**His View:** *Facing Sanders in the Super Bowl came with a lot of things you'd expect—the speed, the talk—but Mills also recalls a few lesser-known aspects of Sanders's game.*

ONE THING ABOUT it when you go against him: You're never going to think you're open because you know he's somewhere close, lurking. You have to be focused on your route and your technique. You've got to get in and out of your cuts. You've got to attack the football. You can't wait on it, or he will make a play on it.

His speed and his makeup speed were what made him different from anybody else. Even if you thought you had him, he always had the ability to make it up. He was going to try to set you up, bait you into something. Sometimes he's going to lock you down, but sometimes he'd try to bait the quarterback to throw the ball. As you can see with the way he analyzes games for the NFL Network, he's a very good student of the game.

Another thing that gave me problems initially was that he was left-handed. He played the majority of the time at the right corner spot. A lot of the routes we ran at Pittsburgh were inside routes, so if you get inside, that route can be pretty easy because that's not their dominant hand. So since he's left-handed and that's his strong hand, he could get in there.

A lot of people don't realize he had a very good jam. Some people say he played soft, because he might not tackle a big guy. But as far as his technique, that was his basic: He'd get up on the line of scrimmage and press you. If someone went up there and went against him, they'd realize how physical he was at the line of scrimmage.

We did a little trash talking out there. I think I caught an out route on him and it was off coverage, and he said, "Aw, that was too easy," and he came up to press. I don't remember exactly what he said, but it was fun. He had the same kind of talk he had back in college. A lot of us guys who came from the state of Florida, we did some trash talking growing up. It was just a part of it. It wasn't curse words or even anything mean. He would tell you what he was going to do, and I'd tell him what I was going to do.

I was really having the game of my life in the Super Bowl, but I tore my ACL with about 10 minutes left. What could have happened if I didn't get injured? I try not to think about it. I played in Dallas my last two years and it always crossed my mind when I was with them. All of them had the ring. I would have loved to have that ring.

# Stan Humphries

## Quarterback

*Teams: Washington Redskins, 1989–91; San Diego Chargers, 1992–97*
*His View: Humphries's Chargers joined the Cowboys on the list of those tor-mented by Sanders in 1994, when he was with San Francisco. Humphries threw an interception that Sanders returned 90 yards for a touchdown in a late-season game, then faced him in the Super Bowl.*

**H**E HAD SUCH great speed and such great anticipation that he would allow guys to get open sometimes, just for a quarterback to think they were open. He knew where his help was, he knew where the ball was probably going to be thrown to make a play on it or intercept it.

You'd never get many plays on him, and if you did it wasn't very often. You had to game plan for him, but at the same time you couldn't allow a guy to take the whole side of the field from you. You at least had to try. That doesn't mean it always works, but you still have to try. Whether it was crossing routes, or pick routes, you would go across the field more than allowing him to stay on the side. He made play after play as far as his abilities to read things.

You couldn't just run out routes, or comeback routes or go routes on his side of the field. You had to run him through traffic. It couldn't just be your receiver against him out on an island. That plays into his game. There were some times you had to do that, and he made plays, like that 90-yard interception for a touchdown.

They played a lot of zone away from him, not to give up big plays. I don't know if we had a lot of big plays against them. It was more of the underneath routes trying to control the ball and keep it away from their offense.

We knew we had to be smart when we were throwing in his area. He's one of those guys that, at any point in the game, whether it was defense, special teams, or offense, he was a guy who could change the momentum of a game in one play. It was just unbelievable.

## Willie Williams

### Cornerback

**Teams:** *Pittsburgh Steelers, 1993–96, 2004–05; Seattle Seahawks, 1997–2003*

**His View:** *Williams went into the Super Bowl expecting to cover Michael Irvin. He ended up covering another eventual Hall of Famer as well, as Sanders hauled in a 47-yard pass against him in the first quarter.*

**I**HAD GREAT COVERAGE, I went over his back and tried to knock the ball down, but he got it. After he caught it, he wasn't used to playing receiver a lot, so I was just trying to hit the ball. But he's a defensive back, too, so he understands what a defensive back is going to try to do. He made a great catch and kept control of the ball.

You watch him on film and he doesn't run great routes. He just runs fast. He'd run deep routes and posts because of his speed. We weren't expecting that skinny post from him because that's Michael Irvin's route.

# Brent Jones

## Tight End

**Team:** *San Francisco 49ers, 1987–97*
**His View:** *Jones knew that having Sanders on his side was the key to San Francisco finally overcoming Dallas to get to the Super Bowl.*

**H**E WAS OUR most important defensive player, because people didn't want to test him and everybody stayed away from him. He kind of cut the field in half. It was something we did not have in the prior NFC Championship games against the Cowboys, so we finally felt like, "We solved this; we can do this and we can win it again." Deion was a great teammate. I wish we could have held on to Deion for another couple years instead of having him go to the Cowboys.

*Extra Point*

# HOME(S) TO AMERICA'S TEAM

The Dallas Cowboys have played in three home stadiums, each packed with peculiarities that left an impression on visiting players.

They played in the Cotton Bowl from 1960 to 1971, when they moved into Texas Stadium in Irving. In 2009, the team opened Cowboys Stadium in Arlington, setting an NFL attendance record with more than 105,000 fans at the opener against the New York Giants.

The enormous new stadium is obviously a far cry from the Cotton Bowl atmosphere Green Bay guard Bill Lueck recalls.

"That was one of the places where I remember Vince Lombardi saying, 'Keep your helmets on, boys, because there are going to be some beer bottles thrown,'" he said. "You didn't know what you were going to get hit with. I never got hit with a beer bottle, but I did get hit with trash. I never turned around to see what it was."

It didn't take long, after Texas Stadium opened in October 1971, for the images to become part of the Dallas lore: the hole in the roof, the sunny and shady spots, and Tom Landry standing stoically on the sideline. It also didn't take long for the foes of America's Team to poke fun at it.

"When they built Texas Stadium with the hole in the roof for America's Team it was supposedly so God could watch the Cowboys," former Eagles cornerback Herm Edwards said. "But we always joked in Philadelphia that that may be partly true, but it's also because their heads are so big they needed that hole so they could fit into the stadium."

Tanya Tucker's song *Texas (When I Die)*, which was a staple in the limited Texas Stadium musical rotation, still haunts former Philadelphia guard Steve Kenney. "They would always play that terrible song in that same stretch of our pre-game warm-ups," he said. "I just remember hearing that ridiculous song and thinking, 'Man, I hate the Cowboys.'"

Jokes and jabs from Philly aside, there was something special about the place for players who grew up hearing Brent Musburger shout, "You are looking live . . ." while watching low-resolution TV aerial footage of Texas Stadium.

"Some stadiums you feel the mystique. You feel the tradition," said former Green Bay nose tackle Gilbert Brown. "You felt like you could look across there and see Tom Landry. That's the same when you come to Lambeau Field. You feel like you can see Lombardi walking up and down that way."

Visiting Texas Stadium for the first time was special to Brent Jones, a 49ers tight end who grew up idolizing the Cowboys.

"I was really kind of moved the first time I was there. This was the place I grew up watching since I was seven or eight," he said.

Texas Stadium was disliked by rivals not just because of the occupants. Many visitors struggled with the "crown," a very gradual rise that made the center of the field slightly higher than the rest of it.

"That crowned field was such an advantage to them," former Giants cornerback Jason Sehorn said. "It messed with your depth perception a little bit, with where you thought the ball was going to end up.

"You looked across at their sideline, and you couldn't see anybody's feet because of where the crown was. We'd watch our quarterback throw high because of it. Learning how to break on that was tough, too. Now, granted, we played on it every single year all 10 of my years, so I got used to it, but not like they did."

Joe Theismann, naturally, had more than a few bad memories in Irving.

"Old Texas Stadium had that hole in the roof because they wanted to make sure God could watch their team and yet the fans could stay dry, or whatever stupid explanation they wanted to give," he said. "I remember lying there so many times looking up at that stupid hole in the roof. There was also a 15–20-yard glaring area where the sun came through, and it literally blinded you when you dropped back to pass."

Some things just don't change when you play the Cowboys, as Theismann pointed out with the new Cowboys' stadium.

"You know what's really funny? Jerry Jones spent $1.2 billion on this stadium, and they have the same lighting problem," he said. "But it's worse. I was on the field at 6 o'clock Dallas time, and there had to be 30 yards of a glare. When you looked toward the end zone, all you could see was sunburst.

"It's a magnificent building. Jerry's done a fantastic job. But I'm thinking, 'If I were to spend $1.2 billion on a stadium that had a 60-yard television screen in it, you'd think I could afford a curtain.'"

*Extra Point*

# FANS OF AMERICA'S TEAM

Brent Jones clearly remembers the day San Francisco finally broke through and beat the Dallas Cowboys for the NFC title.

No, it wasn't the classic 1994 NFC Championship in which he played. It was January 1982, the game known for "The Catch." And while 49ers fans everywhere were rejoicing as Joe Montana threw *the pass* to Dwight Clark, Jones may have been the lone Bay Area teenager who was beside himself. Jones, you see, was a Cowboys fan long before he played for the 49ers.

"I went into a rage," he said. "I was in the tank for a week or two."

Jones was so devoted to Dallas that he wore No. 84 in the pros because of former Cowboys tight end Doug Cosbie. Interviewing former players for this book turned up many more young Cowboys fans who were likewise forced to change their allegiances once they went to work for other NFL teams.

"I grew up in Galveston, Texas, and I was die-hard," said former Cardinals linebacker Eric Hill. "My mom tells the story that when Dallas lost, I cried. I grew up in the Roger Staubach, Tony Dorsett, Robert Newhouse, Randy White era. Here's the funny part about it: To this day, I still pay attention to Dallas."

While growing up in Lubbock and then playing at the University of Texas, former Rams defensive back Jerry Gray also lived and breathed the Dallas Cowboys.

"I was just like everybody else: If they lost on Sunday, you had a bad Monday," Gray said. "It's as if you've been drinking and the next day you have a hangover. But when you win, everybody has a great Monday."

Ernie Mills remembers cheering for the Cowboys as his little brother cheered for the Steelers in the 1978 Super Bowl. "I loved those guys, and I was in there crying after the game," Mills recalled. That sobbing 10-year-old could certainly not imagine he'd go on to play *for* the Steelers *against* the Cowboys in a Super Bowl. (He made up for it, though, by spending his last two years in Dallas.)

Clarence "Sweeny" Williams had the good fortune to be drafted by his favorite team out of college, only to be traded before ever getting to wear the blue star in a game. He was traded to Green Bay, where he spent his entire career.

"Dallas was my team. I'm from Brazoria outside of Houston and went to Prairie View, so I watched them all the time on TV," he said. "I was happy, excited, surprised, and scared when I got drafted by Dallas."

At least Williams got a taste of life as a Cowboy. Other hopefuls never had that much.

"I loved the Cowboys," former Eagles cornerback Herm Edwards said. "I grew up hoping maybe one day I'd play for the Cowboys. After about the second day in Philadelphia, I realized I can't be a Cowboys fan anymore. I couldn't like them that way anymore."

Former Minnesota and Pittsburgh defensive back John Swain figured he'd be a Cowboy when his playing days at the University of Miami were done. So did his sister, who made a huge scrapbook about his college playing days with this label on the front: "Let Your Baby Grow Up to Be a Cowboy."

For Jones, the only disappointment that compared to "The Catch" was not being drafted by Dallas.

"I was just furious," he said. "I talked to Gil Brandt about this at least once every couple years."

# Section 4
# Overtime

## Quotes, Quips, and Tidbits

When you talk to 80 former NFL players, you accumulate all sorts of interesting, insightful, fun, and funny details. Not all of these items fit into the earlier sections of the book perfectly, but they're too good for the cutting-room floor. As these stories and quotes began stacking up, it became clear that they needed a section of the book all to themselves. So here you'll find a fun and disparate collection of nuggets from a wide variety of former Dallas opponents. Unlike the rest of the book, these quotes aren't arranged chronologically. Most of these memories and observations are Cowboys-related, but some are more generally about life in the NFL. This section should bring back some fond memories and provide a little further insight into America's Team.

*Jerry Rice, on the famous saying after Dallas won the 1992 NFC title game:*
"I used to hate that thing Jimmy Johnson said, 'How 'bout them Cowboys!?' I used to *hate* that, and I still do."

*Eric Hill, on his many battles with Daryl Johnston:*
"Let me tell you: We're both responsible for retiring each other, I guarantee. I had neck surgery and he had neck surgery, and I think we put each other out of the league."

*Joe Theismann, on one of the many things that inspired him against Dallas:*
"My high school teammate was Drew Pearson. So you always want to kind of one-up the guy you went to high school with."

217

## FACING AMERICA'S TEAM

*Jack Youngblood, on facing Mike Ditka in his Dallas days:*
"He loved to mess with you. He'd come out and there'd be a four-yard gap—and then he'd earhole you. He'd step down and knock you sideways. I remember telling Mike years afterward, 'My head is *still* hurting where you earholed me.'"

*Gilbert Brown, on he and Nate Newton losing weight after football:*
"I saw Nate on TV and he's like 200 pounds. I was like, 'Wow, he ain't fat no more; look at that.' It's good to see that he's taking his health in the right direction. I told somebody the other day, because I've lost some weight too, but I'm nowhere like Nate: 'We don't have to be that big to choke nobody now, so we're trying to get our sexy on.'"

*Jeff Siemon, on the "shift" the Dallas offensive line used to do before plays:*
"It was unusual to see that the first few times you saw Dallas' offense. It didn't really mean much, but it was probably fun for the fans to see. I think that probably fit into the theme of an offensive team that was known to be sophisticated."

*Aeneas Williams, on the Cowboys' confidence before a game in the 1990s:*
"When they came out and were stretching, I remember vividly Jay Novacek having a toothpick in his mouth. I was just thinking, 'Man, these guys aren't too concerned about us.'"

*Terry Hermeling, on a trick he once tried to beat Jethro Pugh:*
"Jethro was a big grab-and-pull-you-over kind of guy. He was very effective at it, so I figured out how to whip him at that. I used to Vaseline-up the back of my jersey so he couldn't grab me. He would slip because he couldn't get ahold of it. And I actually got tossed because he finally figured out why he couldn't get ahold of me. I had another jersey sewed up nice and tight, and next time I just put silicone on it instead of Vaseline."

*Chuck Foreman, on Thomas "Hollywood" Henderson:*
"He was the first linebacker that I know that could run like a deer. He could run with anybody. He was really good, but he used to talk so damn much. He'd be talking when he was supposed to be doing his job. When he was talking, I was gone."

*Billy Kilmer, on some of his more painful memories against the Cowboys:*
"Jethro Pugh came through on a pass-rush. Just as I let it go, he didn't mean to, but he swiped me right in the jaw. I never wore but one bar on my helmet so he got me in the jaw and knocked me completely out. I remember lying on the grass, smelling that grass, and I didn't want to get up. The hardest hit I took against the Cowboys was when D.D. Lewis pounded me into the ground and separated my right shoulder. I've had a lot of hits against them, but those are the memorable ones."

*Steve Foley, on covering Golden Richards during a trick play in the Super Bowl:*
"Robert Newhouse threw one of the greatest passes. I actually looked up and saw the roof—I never even saw the ball. I heard everybody yelling and I was right there with him. I looked up, and I kind of put my left hand into his face and kind of blocked his vision as I looked back for the ball. It crossed over my head, and as we fell into the end zone, I just saw him with the ball, and I was like, 'Are you kidding me?'"

*Brentson Buckner, on what it feels like for the Steelers to lose to the Cowboys:*
"Losing a Super Bowl hurts, period. But if you're the Steelers and you lose to the Cowboys, that just feels like cutting yourself all over and throwing yourself into a swimming pool full of alcohol. That stings. You're the first Pittsburgh franchise to lose a championship game, then to lose to your greatest rival. Fans in Pittsburgh, they'd rather lose to anybody than the Dallas Cowboys."

*Ted Hendricks, who was 6-foot-7, on tackling 5-foot-10 Robert Newhouse:*
"I remember I missed a tackle on him over on the Dallas sideline and they told me I was getting old. I tried to clothesline him, and he ducked me. The sideline was yelling at me, 'You're losing it, Hendricks.' When he got tackled, I told him to stand up like a man, and when he stood up I found out he could fit under my arm."

*Steve Kenney, on Dick Vermeil's obsession with overcoming the Cowboys:*
"If we had a bad practice or a bad play or a bad quarter, Coach Vermeil would say, 'I bet the Cowboys aren't having a bad practice today.' Or, 'I bet the Cowboys aren't taking the day off.' He would always talk about the Cowboys. We got sick of hearing about the Cowboys. I remember thinking, 'Man, I wish Dallas would take a day off.'"

*Corey Miller, on the attitude of the Cowboys in the 1990s and now:*
"It's kind of hard to see them the way they are now. That swagger and cockiness doesn't seem to exist anymore in Dallas."

*Billy Kilmer, on a game in 1976, two days after being arrested for DWI:*
"Now, I'm really behind the eight ball. I've got to win that game. And so, we go to the game and my wife, Sandy, she was sitting in Cowboys owner Clint Murchison's box. I had a pretty good first half and we're ahead 10–7 at halftime. I throw an interception. Right back, Roger throws us an interception. Then I throw another interception. Then Clint says, 'Hey Sandy, it looks like Billy's sobering up.'"

*Jackie Smith, on joining the Cowboys after 15 years with the rival Cardinals:*
"When I first walked into the room in 1978, my first day there, they booed me. I always seemed to play well against Dallas, and so they remembered that, I guess. But after that, it was all great. I wasn't there long, but it was one of the best parts of my career."

*Ken Houston, on his game-saving tackle of Walt Garrison:*
"When I was traded from the Oilers to the Redskins, they didn't really know anything about the AFL players because the NFL was a superior league. We played the Cowboys on *Monday Night Football* in 1973, and the score was 14–7. They threw a swing pass on the goal line to Walt Garrison. I caught him on the goal line and we won. If he could have put his foot down, he would have scored. That one tackle solidified my career with the Washington Redskins."

*Brentson Buckner, on the Pittsburgh-Dallas Super Bowl in 1995:*
"Both teams respected each other and respected the two franchises and the history we had. There was a mutual respect. Boom, we'd hit each other, look at each other, and just line up and get ready for the next play. There was never any trash talk or anything like that."

*Mark Kelso, on Buffalo's four straight Super Bowl losses, the last two to Dallas:*
"Although we didn't win one, we certainly accomplished something special. I don't know if it'll ever be duplicated, particularly in this era of free agency. I have a box with four Super Bowl rings in it, and a fifth spot waiting for a ring, and we always thought if we kept fighting we'd win one. Unfortunately, that's not the way things happened."

*Jerry Sisemore, on Tom Landry's influence:*
"Coach Landry was a first-class hombre, and that's why all those guys we played against were first-class individuals."

*Steve Preece, on his battles with former Dallas receiver Lance Rentzel:*
"My rookie year, the Saints started me with the entire purpose of hitting him so he never got off the line of scrimmage. We got in a little skirmish and they threw us both out of the game. I think the coaches' plan was to take a rookie who doesn't play and get him thrown out of the game with one of the better receivers. A year later, Lance took me out on a crack block and ended my season. When I came to Los

Angeles in 1973, so did Lance, and we had multiple skirmishes. Then Chuck Knox, in his wisdom, ended up rooming us together on the road and we became really good friends."

*Billy Kilmer, on his reputation for never throwing a spiral:*
"I always said I was the king of the wobbly passes. Somehow, those wobbly passes got to their target. I've seen Tom Brady, I've seen Peyton Manning, I've seen them throw a lot of wobbly passes and nobody says anything about it. They called my wobbly passes ducks. I remember in practice I'd throw and Diron Talbert and those guys would pretend they were shooting it out of the sky."

*Randall Cunningham, on Jerry Jones:*
"He's a winner. The thing I love about Jerry Jones is, he loves his players. And if they fall into a hole, he will go down into the hole, be with them, and bring them back out of the hole. That's the kind of owner you want to play for. You want somebody who loves you, like a Buddy Ryan. Jerry Jones, he gave those players hope."

*Conrad Dobler, comparing today's linemen to those of his era:*
"These big old guys today, come on, let's be serious. It's ridiculous that you can call yourself a professional athlete. Come on, guys. The crack of your ass showing out of your pants. Look professional. Pull your damn pants up."

*Bob Lurtsema, on his tough battles with Dallas:*
"I got in a fight with Walt Garrison one time. His teammate thought what I did was a cheap shot. And from that point on, there was somebody taking an extra crack at me to send me the message that you don't mess with the Dallas Cowboys and Walt Garrison."

*Brent Jones, on facing Dallas days after the Herschel Walker trade:*
"The Cowboys weren't the feared Cowboys then. They had Aikman, but you didn't know if they'd ever be able to put it all the way back together."

*Chris Hanburger, on beating Dallas to reach the 1972 Super Bowl:*
"Nobody expected us to go. We had these folks from some of these equipment companies come by. Some of them gave us these little travel bag–type things and you know what color they were? They were Cowboy colors. I think they got made a little too quick, because I think everybody thought the Cowboys were going."

*Steve Kenney, on how celebrating after plays wasn't accepted in his day:*
"We used to be in film study, and I can remember if a defensive player celebrated after a play, our line coach would say: 'Don't let him get away with that Sunday. If he starts doing all that, you guys take him out.' It was much different. You didn't celebrate. You just did your job."

*Johnnie Gray, on Packers coach Bart Starr copying Dallas' methods:*
"He wanted to be one of the best. And at the time, it was the Dallas Cowboys and the Steelers. When Randy White was taking karate classes, so did we. Here I am, it's the offseason, and I'm at the black belt academy taking tae kwon do classes."

*Charles Mann, on losing to the 1–15 Cowboys in 1989:*
"That's what happens sometimes when you play at home and you're not at the right emotional level. We just went out there and laid a golden egg and gave hapless Dallas their only victory that year."

*Claude Humphrey, on a disagreement with Danny White:*
"The only quarterback the Cowboys had that I ever had a problem with was Danny White. He and I got into a pushing contest up there in Philadelphia. I knocked him down and he didn't like it. He thought it was a little bit late, and it may have been, but it was my job to knock him down. He got a little attitude about it."

# FACING AMERICA'S TEAM

*Na'il Diggs, on rule changes that have made life easier for receivers:*
"Nobody wants to see Deion Sanders locked down on a receiver all game. Nobody wants to watch a shutout. There's fantasy points to be earned. They want to see touchdowns and they want to see scores."

*Chris Hanburger, on players celebrating today:*
"You look at all this nonsense that goes on out on the field today, and God forbid it's ridiculous. They could be behind 25–30 points and they make a tackle or sack somebody and they're going to get up and hop all over the place and everything. If I was a coach, I don't think I'd have any players. They'd all be broke because I'd fine them so much for that kind of nonsense."

*Chuck Foreman, on his famous spin move:*
"You had to know when to and when not to do that, because if you spun at the wrong time, that would not have been a good deal. When I used to spin, I was always looking to get to a place that was open. A lot of guys just spin just to spin."

*Craig Morton, on trying to learn a new offense after Dallas traded him:*
"I was going to an offense that was numbered entirely different than the Cowboys. Landry always numbered the holes odd right and even left, and that's unlike any other system. The holes numbered to the right are always even numbered and to the left it's odd. But since he was a defensive coach, he did it opposite."

*Na'il Diggs, on the Dallas dynasty that won three of four Super Bowls:*
"I think that's part of the sweet history that we all got to take a part of, and I don't think we'll ever see it again."

*Dick Anderson, on the final touchdown catch of Super Bowl VI:*
"I remember after Staubach threw that last touchdown of the game, Coach Shula was just screaming at me then: 'Ditka! You got beat by Ditka!' I remember I joked to Ditka later: 'Mike, you had a great career

and were one of the toughest tight ends in the league. I just wanted you to go out well.'"

*Paul Warfield, on being surprised the Cowboys didn't draft him:*
"I had been scouted very closely by the then–personnel director and one of the shakers and movers of the Cowboy organization, Gil Brandt. And Gil Brandt told me that it was the intention of the Dallas Cowboys to select me. Well, things can change, obviously."

*Charles Mann, on a move used by teammate Jumpy Geathers:*
"Jumpy had a move he would call the forklift. He had real long arms, and he would grab an offensive lineman by the waist, on both sides, like a forklift, and he would actually lift you up in the air. So he didn't grab you with his fingers. He would just grab you by his forearms. Then he would raise you up in the air. You were 300 pounds, and he would lift you up like you didn't weigh anything. And then he would deposit the offensive lineman into the quarterback."

*Clarence "Sweeny" Williams, on getting his nickname:*
"When I was at Prairie View, they didn't call you by your name because they had too many freshmen. They called us, a lot of times, from where we were from. I went to high school in Sweeny, Texas. We had another guy called Tennessee and we had a guy called New York. Even some of my old teammates now, they still call me Sweeny. If somebody calls me Sweeny, I know where they're from."

*Tim Irwin, on an exchange between Bud Grant and a Dallas assistant:*
"The Vikings beat the Cowboys, and the Cowboys had a new strength coach. He shook Bud Grant's hand and said, 'Coach Grant, your guys just beat us.' Bud said: 'We don't have a strength coach. Please don't tell Coach Landry that.'"

*Jim Hart, on Coach Don Coryell's rivalry with Coach George Allen:*
"Don Coryell would always be certain somebody was spying on us. And of course, against the Redskins he knew George Allen *was* spying

on us. He just knew it. Coryell had more respect for Coach Landry than he did against George Allen."

*John Wooten, on his efforts to sway one Dallas fan not to cheer against him:* "I'm a Texan by birth but grew up over in New Mexico. My mom would come over to Dallas and see the games. My mom was a great, great Tom Landry fan. She loved Coach Landry. I used to tell her: 'Whoa, Mom, hold on here. I'm OK with you pulling for the Cowboys when we're not playing them, but when we're playing them, I don't want you pulling for Coach Landry.'"

*Conrad Dobler, on his health after football:* "I've had eight total knee replacements, and I've just had my shoulder replaced. I see these guys coming back from Afghanistan without legs and I realize I don't have a lot of room to bitch. I may not have the greatest knees in the world, but they're still attached. I can still walk. So what do I have to complain about?"

# ACKNOWLEDGEMENTS

**T**HIS BOOK WOULDN'T be possible without the love, patience, and support of my family: Lori, Mason, and Riley. I am blessed to live with these wonderful people and grateful for their willingness to forgive my prolonged absence while they pretended to be interested in football stories from 1974.

Of course I wouldn't have a single football story if it weren't for the gracious assistance of the 80 former players who carved out time from their busy schedules (and sometimes the golf course) to take me on a stroll down memory lane. I admire their love of the game's history, and I appreciate their tolerance for my questions about some of their rougher moments on the field.

Special thanks to my colleague and friend Jaime Aron, who has been an excellent adviser, sharp editor, and patient counselor throughout the reporting and writing of this book. Jaime is one of many current and former sports journalists who were kind enough to allow me to pick their brains. Among the others whose help I deeply appreciate: Charean Williams, Barry Wilner, Schuyler Dixon, and the late Dave Goldberg.

I owe a great debt to the many helpful and dedicated communications professionals who work with, for, or near the NFL. Chief among them: Jilane Rodgers with the NFL Players Association, Chris Schilling with the Pro Football Hall of Fame, Michael Signora with the NFL, Katie Hermsen with the Green Bay Packers, Bob Hagan with the Minnesota Vikings, Frank Kleha with the Atlanta Falcons, Lynne Molyneaux with the Pittsburgh Steelers, Joe Trahan with the Dallas Cowboys, Artis Twyman with the St. Louis Rams, Mike Helm with the Arizona Cardinals, Allie Stoneberg at ESPN, and Andrew Howard at the NFL Network.

Finally, thanks to my many friends and relatives who endured my endless babbling about this book and forgave my withdrawal from society while creating it.